Praise for other work by John D

Pictures from the Water Trade

'Vivid, astute and original' – Philip Oakes, *Sunday Times*

'Joins the tiny handful of books on Japan which display both deep acquaintance and imaginative insight' – Colin Thubron, *Sunday Telegraph*

'One grows into the experience of Japan with Boon/Morley, making random and often acute discoveries as if for oneself' – Anthony Thwaite, *Observer*

The Case of Thomas N

'Distinctly compelling' – *Observer*

'The book is formal and detached, markedly different from run-of-the-mill fictional outpourings, and a reminder of the European origins of the psychological novel. It is an achievement worthy of considerable respect' – Anita Brookner, *Spectator*

In the Labyrinth

'Provokes deep sad thoughts upon the human condition' – *Literary Review*

'Extremely well written and constructed . . . The dispassionate, observant tone of the book gives great power to its sad and appalling testimony, a testament to cruelty, fear and ignorance that continues today at an even harsher level in many of the world's prisons' – *The Times*

Previously resident in Singapore, England and Japan, John David Morley now lives in Germany. Besides writing books and journalism, he works as a translator and interpreter.

ENCOUNTERS

JOHN DAVID MORLEY

BLOOMSBURY

First published in Great Britain 1990
Bloomsbury Publishing Ltd, 2 Soho Square, London WIV 5DE

Copyright © John David Morley 1984, 1985, 1986, 1987, 1988, 1989
This collection © John David Morley 1990

A CIP catalogue record for this book
is available from the British Library

ISBN 0 7475 0600 0

10 9 8 7 6 5 4 3 2 1

Typeset by Hewer Text Composition Services, Edinburgh
Printed and bound in Great Britain by Richard Clay Ltd, Bungay, Suffolk

For Anthony Holden

Vien dentro e lo saprai:
diverse istorielle che accadute mi
son dacche partisti –

ACKNOWLEDGMENTS

Acknowledgments are due to the following publications in which some of the pieces in this book have appeared previously: *New York Times* (A Horizontal Culture); *Departures* (Sweet Potato Seller, In Celebration); *Traveler* (The Haute Route); *Sunday Times Magazine* (The Japanese with the Green Eyes, The Chairman, The Pencil Makers, The Lady Vanishes, New Clothes for Old, A Magic Touch, Germany Incorporated); *Observer Magazine* (Poker Fez); *Vanity Fair* (Lament for the Makaris); *Saison* (Pirate Night Aboard the Deli Sarpa).

CONTENTS

Places

CLEAN, GREEN, HIGH-RISE KAMPONG   3
Singapore Revisited

A HORIZONTAL CULTURE   16
Beginners' Guide to Japan

SWEET POTATO SELLER, HIGH-TECH
   AKIHABARA STORE   20
Tokyo

IN CELEBRATION   31
Munich

THE DECLINE OF GERMANY'S INDUSTRIAL
   HEARTLAND   42
The Ruhrgebiet

PIRATE NIGHT ABOARD THE DELI SARPA   52
Package-cruising the Aegean on a Turkish Junk

TWO AND A HALF THOUSAND MILES ON
   THE DANUBE   61
From Vienna to the Black Sea and Back

THE HAUTE ROUTE   73
A Ski Crossing of the Alps

People

THE JAPANESE WITH THE GREEN EYES   89
Akio Morita, Alias Mr Sony

THE CHAIR MAN   104
Rolf Fehlbaum and his Museum

The Pencil Makers 109
Faber-Castell

The Lady Vanishes 118
Veruschka, Body Painter

New Clothes For Old 125
The Rag Trade in Prato

A Magic Touch 133
The World Magic Congress in Madrid

Poker Fez 144
Amarillo Slim and Co. at the All Moroccan Championship

Germany Incorporated 152
Student Duelling Fraternities

The Sins Of The Fathers 166
The Lost Generation of Niklas Frank

The Grand Illusionist 175
On the Centenary of the Death of Ludwig II

Lament For The Makaris 191
In Memory of Richard Burton

PLACES

CLEAN, GREEN HIGH-RISE KAMPONG
Singapore Revisited

I was born in something of a hurry on a bench in a third-class Chinese ward at the Kandang Kerbau Maternity Hospital, a couple of blocks from a now dilapidated Burmese Buddhist temple in Kinta Road and within wailing distance of the Sri Veeramakaliamman Temple, which has worn rather better. The statues of Siva's wife adorning the temple show a fiercely resolute woman, flanked by lions, with a wide stare and swollen, gourd-like belly that might have taken their cue as much from the nearby maternity hospital as from the sensuous hands of the Bengali craftsmen who moulded her. Little India, as the neighbourhood is known, has changed a little. The Foochow Methodist Church, still loitering hopefully on Race Course Road, was then doing business in a Crown Colony where Lee Kuan Yew was an unknown quantity still cutting his considerable political teeth and nobody had heard of Kentucky Fried Chicken or of the Republic of Singapore.

Forty years on, my second incarnation in Singapore is experienced not as a brave new citizen of the world but as a middle-aged tourist suspended in now much briefer transit. Comparisons are difficult, but this time the arrival seems a lot more comfortable, lubricated by the efficient midwifery of Changi airport officials who deliver me from an exquisite reservoir of coolness to the street outside in twenty minutes. This is where the tropics begin, right here, one degree north of the equator, with a humidity averaging eighty-five but often approaching one hundred percent. I feel I am walking through a wall, my body

3

deliciously bruised by an air I can no longer ignore because it is always palpable to my skin.

There are several ways of absorbing a tropical climate. One is with air-conditioning, which entirely shuts it out. Another is with agreeable eddies of air generated by old-fashioned ceiling fans, which make you want to remain sitting in a rattan chair with a glass of gin for ever. And the other is with nothing between you and it at all, in sweaty, stupefying, no-holds-barred symbiosis.

Very soon after my arrival I am fortunate enough to visit an expatriate couple whose way of life in a restored colonial house, shortly to be torn down, alas, like so many older buildings in Singapore, demonstrates all three Climate Combat Methods in convincing combination. The house also demonstrates the pleasure of living with local scents and sounds reaching luxuriantly through your open window, where there is a view down over the tops of trees and industrial docklands, remote enough to appear picturesque, to a glittering island-sprinkled sea.

I want all of these things, and I can get many of them at Raffles Hotel. Some people say that Raffles is an acquired taste. Others say that it is not a taste at all. The grand old lady of Singapore's hotels, now a hundred and one years old, makes no attempt to conceal her age; and she has lived raucously in an intemperate climate. She had her face painted for the centenary celebrations and can still dazzle passing visitors with a stagey splendour; underneath the façade she is falling apart. Major surgery is now planned to restore the diva to her former greatness, but charm may not be something you can operate on. In deference to her age and all too human frailties I shall pass over the furnishings, plumbing, decor etc. in silence. Forget the room. Open the door and look out.

A long, shady, white-bordered walk encloses the wonderful tropical garden of the Palm Court. Early in the morning, when the trees are still crackling in the aftermath of a monsoon rainstorm and crepuscular light, rising vertically from the horizon to the zenith, surprises me every time with the suddenness of day,

4

I lean over the balustrade with all my senses poised to absorb the garden below in its morning freshness. Between the spokes of the Traveller's palms, standing like half-splayed fans which somehow I am always expecting will open, I glimpse the orange flame of the flowering bush known as Musanda Dona Luz, Mistress of Light; a haze of bougainvillea; purple and white orchids in hanging baskets, garlands of colour so delicate that it seems to detach itself and float, a disembodied essence of flower. Bolder, more startling, the scarlet and yellow blossoms bursting from the dark green leaves of the frangipani whose scent lingers heavily in the humid air; a cloying, almost an oppressive scent with the ambiguity of ripeness and decay that I feel to be inherent in so much of tropical life.

At breakfast, under a gallery of sound provided by caged singing birds, I meet the first thing in Singapore to which I take an instant, incurable dislike. It is the *Straits Times*, purportedly a newspaper, effectively a government bulletin. Frequently it opens its mouth to be magisterial and nannyish ('Are you taking calcium carbonate to help prevent osteoporosis?'), or to bare its fangs ('High Court ruling means gallows for Hong Kong man'), and occasionally laying on chilling, leprous hands ('Schoolchildren will be taught the concepts of Civil Defence in a fun way'). There is a lot of talk about a Marxist Conspiracy in May this year when sixteen people were detained without trial under the Internal Security Act (ISA), some of whom are still in jail.

Leaving them in jail, I go out to tour the island. I have already toured its statistics and had a bird's-eye view as I came in to land. It is a heart-shaped island roughly thirty kilometres wide and forty-two long, with an area of only five hundred and seventy square kilometres where over two and a half million people live. Three quarters of them are Chinese. Malays weigh in at fifteen percent, Indians at six point four percent, around two percent are accounted for by the mysterious ethnic entity of Others. Between them they subscribe to the religions of

Islam, Buddhism, Christianity, Hinduism, Sikhism and Judaism. These are the statistics sketching the island republic's richly colourful multi-cultural community. Alternatively, depending on how adroitly it is governed, they also supply the ingredients of a lurid multi-racial explosion. It puts into perspective why the British introduced ISA in the first place, and why Prime Minister Lee Kuan Yew and his People's Action Party, both in office since 1959, have remained so reluctant to remove this loincloth of their colonial heritage in a politically more liberal age.

But first things first: the Singaporeans under the visionary guidance of Lee have transformed their island into a garden city. Clean and Green was the name of the game they began in the 1960s – clean and green it has become. In the few surviving old parts of town such as the Arab Street district, Little India and Chinatown you stroll gratefully in the shade of quaint, crumbling arcades, known locally as Five Foot Ways, but everywhere else the service of shade is supplied by avenues of trees. Walking at midday a couple of miles along Orchard Road, famous for its lavish hotels, labyrinthine shopping emporia and illegal touts, hawking at bargain prices imitations of almost any brand product you want, I do not need my topee because I am never exposed to the sun. Driving across the island from north to south along the six-lane expressway in half an hour, or slightly longer from east to west, I admire the boxes of bougainvillea flowering on concrete flyovers, the superbly groomed grass verges, the green miles of Rain tree and the rich vegetation that continue all the way along the finest stretch of urban landscaping I think I have ever seen.

The modern Singapore provides a demonstration of how to domesticate the tropics. It's not the place to go if you're looking for the authentic experience of equatorial rain forest. Mini-jungle is still available in the centre of the island at the Bukit Timah Reserve. Don't Kill the Animals, says a notice at the jungle admission gate; my priority is that the animals don't kill me. I am armed with an umbrella, ostensibly in case of rain, secretly in case of snakes. But apart from the steady whine of cicadas and the chatter of children on school outings the jungle is disappointingly quiet. The cobra and the reticulated python, if they are here, have no intention of letting me know. The only animal I see is an ant. My umbrella is no use even when it rains, for by the time the rain has reached me through a hundred and fifty feet of foliage it is a negligible increment to the rivulets of moisture I have already generated myself.

I find a more satisfying jungle experience at the Botanic Gardens, where nature – and I am beginning to recognise this as the theme of Singapore – is accommodated by art. The pocket edition of primary forest, concentrated in only four hectares, is strikingly more *jungly* than nature's complete works.

Liana as thick as my arm make Tarzan credible in the Botanic Gardens, whereas the shoddily manufactured article in the Reserve would be contemplated as a means of conveyance only by a suicidal eccentric. Vast trees with shaggy bark and of truly equatorial girth tower briefly and soar out of sight at tertiary levels of foliage; at ground level, the sward of dense, matted vegetation rolls up on either side of the swept paths I walk like a wake of green waves. Sumptuous tropical plants are here enhanced by the pleasure of learning their exotic names – the Cannon Ball Tree, whose musky fragrance issues from long inflorescences groping like tentacles out of its trunk, the Yellow Flame Tree and the Elephant's-Ear Tree, the Morning Glory and the lovely Rose of Venezuela.

Beach life is the same kind of synthetic experience as the jungle. Singapore's strands are dismal by shimmering south-east Asian standards, and inshore waters, although they may be relatively pollution-free, don't look particularly clean. At the tourist island of Sentosa tropical life is packaged and recreated under glass: most of the butterflies are in the Insectarium, the only coral is in the Coralarium. Sentosa may be able to claim the distinction of being the only place in the world where you approach your swim in an island lagoon via cable car and monorail. The sand looks more inviting here. It has been imported from Malaysia.

In search of a boat that will take me to the most southern group of islands within the port limits of Singapore I spend a morning snooping around Clifford Pier. It is here I meet the engaging and maybe engagable Ah Hee. Ah Hee is a nautical man with what looks like a seaworthy craft and a helmsman's certificate to prove he can drive it, but his fast talk, slick hair and natty suede shoes give him more the air of a racecourse bookie.

While we negotiate he ushers me through the bustle of the pier, shows me the junks and the broad-bottomed bumboats that service the ships at anchor in the harbour, the skiffs poled by ancient Malays who in turn service the bumboats, the corners of the jetty where Chinese crews with bruised faces squat on their heels and gamble, naturally against the law, and by the time we are through I am so delighted with Ah Hee's savvy and tall yarns that I find his asking price perfectly reasonable. How about deposit, huh, front money now, says Ah Hee, talking faster. No deposit, say I. Ah Hee grins, and solemnly we pledge our agreement in Roman and Chinese scripts on the reverse side of his beautifully tailored business card.

Our destination is Pulau Seking, as it appears on my map, or Sakeng, as it appears on Ah Hee's. Whatever its name, the tiny island accommodates a kampong, a traditional Malay village perched on stilts extending into the water, which in Singapore is soon going to be another extinguished species. The journey out there makes clear why.

Standing on deck, I see on the southern horizon the low-slung, dark green islands of Indonesia, for me as redolent of Conradian mystery and imagination as the Tiffin Room at Raffles is of the sultry tales of Maugham and Kipling, but something prompts me to turn round. Much closer in place and time is the Manhattan-style skyline of the shore behind me. We are chugging along the waterfront of the busiest port in the world, which can turn a tanker round in eight hours. We can chug on, Ah Hee's antique diesel engine permitting, all the way to Indonesia, and still be dominated in a flat expanse of sea by that towering twenty-first century skyline etched against the sky.

I feel it there behind me as we coast past the tip of Pulau Bukum, an offshore industrial site where Shell operates refineries, and draw in toward our palm-topped kampong island. Half a mile away it still looks magical, a floating village on stilts as dainty as a flock of flamingo legs. Closer in, I identify goats rummaging in garbage underneath the platforms those legs support, and corrugated iron roofs on top of them.

It is an arid, stony, glass-strewn island. Nothing much that is eatable grows on it. Nobody can make a living here, not even from fishing. The villagers have to commute to work by boat, as do the few children who go to school, island-hopping from their kampong to the Shell refinery and from there to Singapore. Guides with loudhailers, ripping open the villagers' Sunday morning quiet, conduct Chinese tourists from the main island who come to peer inquisitively into the privacy of their archaic lives. It is unsurprising that they are wary and incommunicative.

Singapore's two and a half million people generate a twenty billion dollar economy, which for the most part is accounted for by oil and petroleum products, banking and fund management expertise, telecommunications, electronics, fabricated metal and peripheral computer products. It is not the sort of economy that can be generated out of a Malay kampong. The air-conditioned high-rise buildings in which many Singaporeans work are complemented by the high-rise tenements in which around eighty-five percent of them live. The Housing and Development Board's construction projects are eating into the virgin forest still left in remoter corners of the island as fast as the government can plant trees along new sections of the Pan-Island Expressway.

I see this advance of urbanisation most impressively when

JOHN DAVID MORLEY

I look at it across the Straits of Johore from Malaysia. The northern coastline of Singapore is still green, but the outposts of urban development have already marched to the crest of the hill and are looking hungrily down. The garden city of the Singaporeans will soon become a garden housing estate, occupying the entire island. For three million visitors who now arrive there annually, normally spending a few days to repair body and mind and be wonderfully looked after, it has already begun to resemble a sort of extension of Changi airport lounge.

Singapore has always been the port of call between east and west. There may be holiday destinations more exciting and exotic, but in an age of trans-world jet travel the need for a halfway resting house has grown rather than diminished, and as such the city is unsurpassed. It is a place to switch off and relax, to launch out on bargain shopping sprees – and to eat. After a multi-culinary, two-week odyssey through the melting-pot of Singapore, challenging my palate and digestive functions without imposing the least strain on either, I conclude that night for night, meal for meal, I have consistently dined better here than anywhere else in the world.

For me and many of my fellow tourists, judging by their numbers, the real pleasure of Singaporean food is eating it outdoors, along with the locals, at one of the dozens of hawker centres all over town. The food is cheap, choice, and encyclopaedic in its variety – Indian dishes steamed and grilled from an entire subcontinent (with a tendency to get hotter the further you eat your way south), Malay, Indonesian and Chinese, incorporating Hokkien, Hakka, Hainanese, Sichuan, Shanghainese, Cantonese and Peking specialities, and Singapore's local hybrid, a blend of several Asian cuisines, which is known as Straits Chinese.

I start off, sedately, at the Satay Club, whose waterfront extension is known as the Padang, on Queen Elizabeth Walk.

Satay is barbecued meat on sticks, similar to Japanese yakitori, served with spiced sauces and available at all the hawker centres I sample: at Roti John, opposite the Botanic Gardens, the Pasir Panjang Road hawker centre (which I particularly recommend for plain, home-style Malay cooking), the East Coast Road Seafood Centre (for anything edible that swims or crawls in the seven seas), the Maxwell Market just opposite the original jinrikisha station at the corner of Tanjong Pagar and Neil Road, and the terrific centre at Newton Circus, that apotheosis of the dense, compounded odours, colours, sights, sounds and the clamorous pitch of stall owners which are so characteristic of hawker centres.

There are surprisingly few Malay restaurants in Singapore, but the instinct of my own nose, now thoroughly attuned, and the advice of one of my favourite receptionists at Raffles, whose grandeur of girth substantiates his opinions on eating matters, immediately lead me to the best. Located at 36 Emerald Hill Road, it is Aziza's Restaurant, whose eponymous owner, herself an eater of stature, claims to run the only place in town serving the original noodle-like bread known as Roti Renjis. In a small restaurant with intimate atmosphere I sample Sambal Goreng ('captivating mixture of liver, onions, shrimps, mutton in zesty, herby sauce'), Kacang Panjang Goreng ('long-bean fried with scampi') and Sotong Berkelar (squid, made accessible in excellent spicy sauce), which with drinks amounts to just under nineteen dollars.

And this isn't cheap by local standards. At the Victory Restaurant on North Bridge Road, one of a triplet of Indian restaurants located side by side and serving identical food on the principle that this will somehow ensure a fair share of business, I dispatch a capacious snack of Murtabak - white flour filled with onions, meat or chicken and fried pancake-style - for a ridiculous three dollars. Well inside my day's budget, a pennant of Victory onions fluttering almost visibly on my breath, I stride out to take possession of the tropical night spots.

By chance, perhaps, my visit to Singapore coincides with what the *Straits Times* claims to be the first survey of female sexuality ever conducted in my native town. Even harder to believe are the survey's results, reported by the paper in its bland, magisterial manner, to the effect that ninety-seven percent of the marriages annulled last year were on grounds of non-consummation, an omission which gynaecologist-researcher Dr Atputharajah attributes to the startling fact that, 'sex is a topic surrounded by myth, taboo and awe . . . couples don't know where to put what.'

I ponder on Dr Atputharajah's words, I ponder on the advisability of eating onions prior to night club visits, as I sit in the cavernous twilight of the Lido Palace at the Glass Hotel Shopping Centre where for the past half hour the staff-clientele ratio has remained constant at twenty to one. I ponder them again at the Instant Cultural Show I view at Raffles (also available at the Mandarin and the Hyatt Regency), which is less a night-club show than a sort of ad for the successful fusion, or knowing where to put what, of Singapore's instant multi-cultural community. The Chinese Ribbon Dance, the Malay Village Dance, the Indian Pot Dance . . . there is something here that is surrounded by myth, taboo and awe, but it definitely ain't sex. And I begin to wonder if the dearth of conjugal nightlife in Singapore, indeed, of any discernible night-life at all, might benefit just a little from relaxing the stringent censorship laws that ban naked bodies from page, stage and screen and keep everyone in the dark.

After a week in the city's oldest hotel I move into its newest, which at the time of writing is the Oriental Singapore. Here I am living on reclaimed land. From the thirteenth storey I look down on the concrete flyover spanning the Geylang river to the south; and to the east, likewise on reclaimed land, at the organ-pipe arrangement of Bedok New Town. I have a view outside; but outside seems strangely irrelevant. The true force behind the design of this hotel, as of many of the modern, stylish, well-serviced hotels I have looked into here, is centripetal: one is drawn inwards, to the cool twilight interiors of enclosed spaces, to the shops, banks, restaurants, bars and purveyors of every conceivable service, arranged in tiers around a quarter-circle atrium that soars twenty-one storeys high.

My equatorial environment becomes marginal, almost non-existent. I can keep my cool all day and night. I can, and unless I spend a lot of time on the telephone negotiating with the management I *have* to, because I don't have a key to unlock my window. The symphony of tropical heat, scents and sounds is scored down to a faint intermezzo between alighting from air-conditioned cabs and entering air-conditioned hotels, shopping emporia and government offices, where I go to seek confirmation of rumours suggesting that Lee may be losing his marbles.

His Graduate Mothers Scheme, for example, floated a couple of years back in an attempt to speed up the production line of Singaporean babies that previous government controls had too effectively slowed down, encouraged the idea that better educated women should have seeded priority because they would yield more intelligent children. And quite recently he has been thinking out loud on the subject of polygamy as a form of marriage his insular people might like to consider. I gather this is just Lee's style of government by unofficial referendum. He launches a lot of kites, and some of them never get off the ground.

The cameos of Singapore I have recorded and will treasure have not been gleaned from the sparkling city of high buildings, high government and high quality of life that has spread out and up from the site where Stamford Raffles first landed one hundred and seventy years ago. There's not much gleaning to do in streets so immaculately swept. I will remember the Arabs and swarthy bearded Sikhs, in gowns and turbans of luminous whiteness, sipping coffee and talking softly under the arcades of rickety two-storey houses with sun-bleached tiles in Bussorah Street;

the miraculous garland-maker in Little India, conjuring flower chains out of the air as he twined gold-white buds of jasmine around strips of fibre from the banana tree and knotted orchids at the base; the dhobi in Norris Road, the last in Singapore, where three ageing, slow-speeched men still boil laundry in a cauldron and punish it in stone troughs for their few fastidious customers; Bok Chee Yong, the calligrapher-cum-fortune-teller in Chinatown, whose ideograms transliterated my name to mean Fun Horse Forest and told me I'd live to be seventy-three with a bonus of five years thrown in if I did charitable works; Meow Choon Foh Yit Kee, whose pharmacy just down the road at 134 Telok Ayer Street sells antelope horn for cooling fever, sea-horse and sea-dragon for clearing up acne, dinosaur fossil from China (in every sense an arresting treatment for people whose problem is kidney debility or premature ejaculation), and galvanic compounds, in an adjacent drawer, of dog, tiger, reindeer or seal penis for people whose problem is no ejaculation at all. I purchase uncontroversial sachets of asthma powder.

In the modern Singapore, however, Chinatown, the Arab Street district and the Little India where I was born have become quaint anachronisms, and I am aware that my curiosity in the customs of people living in condemned buildings acquires an element of voyeurism. Nothing epitomises this better than the grotesque trishaw ride I take the evening I arrive, artificially marooned on three wheels of antiquity, down the superslow inside lane of an inner-city expressway dominated by international banks and the seventy-three storey Westin Stamford, the tallest hotel in the world. Alighting at the Victoria Memorial Hall I wander between the few elegant buildings preserved from colonial days, and pass on up to the old Christian cemetery at the gates of Fort Canning Park.

A crescent moon is riding buoyantly up the sky, by the fading light of day I can just decipher the names of the earliest settlers who were buried here a hundred and fifty years ago. It is a sentimental journey into the past. But two weeks later, when

ENCOUNTERS

I take a last walk under bracelets of golden light announcing the coming of Christmas to Orchard Road, I have learned that the crescent moon with five white stars is the emblem on the flag of Singapore, representing a young nation, air-conditioned, and unmistakably on the ascendant.

A HORIZONTAL CULTURE
Beginners' Guide to Japan

A pril and May, the season of the cherry blossoms, and September and October, the time of the maple colours, are traditionally thought of as the ideal time to visit Japan. But the traveller who seeks to get to know something of the people of Japan as well as the usual tourist sights may prefer to submit voluntarily to the humidity of summer or the rigours of winter. Merely by being in the country at the wrong time of year such a traveller can become part of a community – the community that forms in opposition to an uncomfortable climate.

Air-conditioned and centrally heated hotels must be avoided for this reason. Apply to the Japan Travel Bureau for a room in the kind of traditional Japanese inn known as ryokan. Low-rise ryokan will introduce you to customs that survive everywhere in daily life in Japan except in hotels. You will take off your shoes in the porch and venture down a corridor with a polished wooden floor in slippers kindly supplied by the house. In deference to the tatami, the plaited rush floor covering, you will leave the slippers outside your room and rediscover the pleasure of moving around on stockinged feet. You will sit on the tatami and you will also sleep on it. Most Japanese still do. Some of them even sleep on the floor beside their bed.

Living in a ryokan helps to familiarise one with a low-rise culture whose esthetics can only be appreciated on a horizontal plane. This remains the case even in modern apartment blocks; the tenth floor is still the floor rather than the tenth. Your eyes are more nearly on a level with the objects around you. I have always felt that this closeness to the floor must have helped to shape the bedrock egalitarianism of Japanese society. Before going to a department store to purchase typical japonaiserie such as pottery or a lacquered table it is a good idea to have already lived with these things at their indigenous level. A stay in a ryokan makes that possible.

Sweltering in your room on a sultry August evening you will find local remedies can give the best relief. Ask your unfailingly courteous hosts for a soothing glass of mugi-cha, the cold barley tea always found in Japanese refrigerators in summer. Listen for the occasional tinkling of the furin, the wind bell that you prudently bought on the day of your arrival and hung at the window, and ponder the artful psychology of amplifying even the faintest stirring of a breeze as an acoustic perception that will deceive your nervous system into producing a sensation of coolness.

These are modest pleasures, to be sure, but modesty is the essence of the Japanese experience.

The Japanese have learned to manoeuvre within a small space. The few objects in their austerely furnished rooms can breathe and come to life. The habitual exercise of restraint in their consumption of food, energy, leisure and space allows them to be genuinely satisfied with less. At the core of a modern consumer society, despite its extravagant and glittering surface, the austerity remains unchanged.

At the ryokan it is unlikely that anyone will speak intelligible English. And you, presumably, speak no Japanese. This is an advantage. You will be spared the elaborate formalities of courtesy language. Deprived of verbal communication, the Japanese will resort to sign language and pantomime, and you will respond in kind. These sign games will be an occasion for shared laughter. The reserve towards strangers that is required by Japanese etiquette already begins to thaw. Your mutual language deficit is in reality a cloak of invisibility, allowing you to cross the threshold of social protocol unquestioned.

The Japanese are most obviously released from the requirements of protocol under three circumstances: when they are under the influence of alcohol, when they take off their clothes, and when they are in the privacy of their home. Let us consider the first circumstance.

Bars in Japan belong to a bohemian world colloquially known as the water trade. There is a suggestion of dilution in this name that may not appeal to those who like their bourbon straight, but rest assured, the water trade is an honest purveyor of honest liquor. It is also absolutely safe (although women may find their evening less strenuous if accompanied by a male escort). Without any misgivings you can push aside those intriguing navy-blue curtains, that frosted glass door, and step inside. You will find yourself in an alternative culture, almost a different world.

Order your drink, sit back, and keep your eyes wide open. You are a foreigner. Exploit the bonus. Someone will want to talk to you, if only to try out his English. Have your business card ready. In the meantime there is plenty to observe. Men will be taking off their jackets, unbuttoning their collars and loosening their ties. This is a sure sign that they are also beginning to loosen their tongues. They will pass, quite rapidly, through the stages of amiable communicativeness and hilarity to a more or less glazed stupefaction at the end of the evening, for the water trade is where the strain of Japanese society is borne. The shirt-tails of informality show here.

From Kagoshima in the south to Sapporo in the north, any one of the tens of thousands of bars in any of Japan's cities will provide a suitable venue for your initiation into the Japanese mind. In the no man's land of the water trade, in its confidential anonymity, you will see and hear a great deal more than on the broad tourist highways that take in the monuments and miss the details.

A more restful alternative to the openings offered by the water trade can be sought at one of Japan's delightful thermal springs, which are known as onsen. Most are to be found on the northernmost island of Hokkaido and in the northern region of the main island, Honshu. Thermal springs with a sophisticated, still urban flair can be found closer to the capital at Atami or Hakone, only a couple of hours by rail from Tokyo, but it is the rural calm of onsen villages perched in the mountains, with magnificent scenic views, that the discerning tourist will want to experience as a contrast to the hectic cities.

There is a Japanese saying that 'one takes off one's clothes to talk'. Company outings to thermal springs are arranged for just this purpose. Senior and junior staff, mingling naked in steaming waters, can explore relationships with a frankness that the formality of their society forbids elsewhere. This loophole can equally be exploited by foreigners.

Equipped with nothing but a small white towel, you can enter a magical floating world from which the bathers' shield of reserve has been banished along with their clothes. In these quieter byways of the water trade the atmosphere is more civilised, in its own way intoxicating, not quite real, but in a literal sense more sober than the bars in the city. In the outdoor thermal springs known as rotenburo you can invite your fellow bathers to share a flask of sake while enjoying the scenery, or arrange to meet for a meal afterwards in the privacy of your room.

You will become acquainted with people who will invite you into their homes. They will extend the invitation modestly, almost apologetically, because you come from a country with a lot of space and their own homes are very small. But you are prepared for that. Your stay in a ryokan has persuaded you that small is beautiful is not merely a slogan. In Japan it is a whole way of life.

SWEET POTATO SELLER,
HIGH-TECH AKIHABARA STORE
Tokyo

The beginners' Japanese classes at the Language Research Institute didn't start for another week, so there would be time for a preliminary circumnavigation of Tokyo, an attempt to find my bearings in what at first sight seemed to be an impossibly complex city. A friend from the Philippines, who had been in the country for a year and already sounded impressively fluent in the language, accompanied me to the local station on the Ikegami line, punched all the right buttons on the ticket vending machine and explained how to get to Shibuya. He lent me a beginners' map of the city and the subway system, with names conveniently marked in Japanese script and Roman letters. Otherwise all I needed was a pocketful of small change, my five senses, admittedly jet-lagged, but more or less in working order; and a notebook to record those first impressions that would begin to fade as I became more familiar with my surroundings, and soon be irrecoverable.

By Tokyo standards, the suburb of Meguro Ward where the foreign students' hall of residence was located was out in the boondocks when compared with the terrific street life of Shibuya. Emerging haphazardly from one of the station's dozen exits, I found the onslaught of strange impressions immediate and overpowering: shop signs branching above my head as if I were in some kind of dense urban wood, stores below selling often unidentifiable goods, coffee shops featuring Space Raider games between rubber plants, plastic food in the display windows of restaurants, policemen kennelled in boxes at busy junctions, vending machines offering pink milk and pornography, armoured vans with people in helmets making impassioned speeches to which nobody listened, artificial flowers still adorning parks whose trees had lost their natural blossom, a playground where a solitary blue-suited man sat on a swing, mid-morning golfers driving in netted roof-top cages, noodle stalls, massage parlours, shoeshine slaves on a sidewalk beneath the never-ending thunder of a railway bridge, high fashion in highrise department stores bearing curious English names, waste-disposal cans discriminated in English TRASH – and people, boys and girls, men and women, young people flowing from every cranny of the horizon, a brilliant, volatile crowd at a fast-moving pace that never seemed to slacken until I turned into the park marked on my map between the Embassy of Bulgaria and the Turkish Embassy, and headed for Meiji Jingu shrine.

At the shrine I saw the Shinto ritual of clapping hands; an old couple, wizened faces in profile, fingertips touching in what seemed to be a prayer. But the majority of the Japanese visitors were more interested in photographing each other. I watched them take their snapshots, adjust a smile, enshrine a pose, wondering what they felt and saw. Was this archaic splendour theirs? Did they come to acknowledge a heritage? Idling for the course of an hour and a couple of hundred visitors, I couldn't find much evidence. They were tourists like myself, but tourists who didn't seem to be looking at what they had come to visit. Perhaps it was too familiar. Not what the eye remembered, because it didn't need to, but what the camera recorded, because it documented the occasion – perhaps this was what mattered to them. Later, in pursuit of this instinctive perception, I would ignore the prayerful hands and tapering eyelids in profile, discovering instead that the modern image of the Japanese was not one of pilgrims but of tourists on a visit to their own past.

More of the past that afternoon, when across the moat surrounding the Imperial Palace I caught a glimpse, between the trees, of terraced roofs and sweeping eaves ending in knobbly cornices, like horns, which gently seemed to toss the sky; and two blocks away, with memories of Wall Street as one walked through Marunouchi, more of the present: a bank without any tellers in it doing brisk lunch-hour business. This part of town catered for a sleeker clientele; with closer-cropped hair, suits beneath it that had not more but discreeter stripes. At lunch the stripes converged in a buck-wheat noodle restaurant opposite the bank. Standing room only, heads bowed, one hand cupping a bowl a few inches from lips, the other levering chopsticks with an absolute economy of movement within an absolute economy of space – attaché cases between standing-room-only legs, the gleam of prosperity on highly polished shoes.

I was told I had to see it, so I got up at dawn to snatch angles of the blueish, raucous morning at the fish market in Tsukiji, where men in boots, sometimes barefoot in wooden clogs, hauled mackerel and giant tuna across the reeking floor of a morgue; later I revived my numb senses in a stiff spring breeze off the living sea, sweeping inland across Tokyo Bay and bringing coal dust, the lowing of ships' horns, the garbled tang of the outlying ocean to Harumi's wharves. I noticed the curious footwear of longshoremen and construction workers, knee-high moccasins, supple-soled and cobbled like a glove to give precision to the toeholds of feet dancing slowly along girders at dizzy heights overhead. This stealthy, probing movement of the construction workers' gloved feet was still in my mind when I recrossed the Sumida River that afternoon on my way to the Kabuki-za. I thought I recognised it, and wondered if this was where it had originated, in the smooth seeking motion of the Kabuki actor's white-stockinged feet, sliding across the stage floor as if they had their own economy of purpose, the same kind of physical intelligence that here seemed to be localised in the soles of an actor's feet.

ENCOUNTERS

Higher at sunset, on a rare evening when the air had the clarity of the sound of a bell, with visibility extending far beyond the city limits, I was surprised by an apparition of Mount Fuji from the top of Tokyo Tower. In the haze of distance the white summit of the mountain seemed to detach itself from any terrestrial base and to levitate in the sky. Throughout the gradually darkening twilight I watched the apparition fade, lights spring up in the dark city below like a carpet of night flowers.

For most of that first week I looped the city on the Yamanote Line, from Tabata in the north to Shinagawa in the south, getting off to spend a little time in the precincts of every station. At Nishi-Nippori I ate for two dollars curried rice with pickles in the murderous bustle of midday, and would remember without the assistance of my notes the sallow, exhausted, indefatigably cheerful face of the young man who ladled curry all day in one steaming square yard between his pots and his counter. Space didn't seem to get any bigger, but possibly better appointed, undeniably more expensive, the further the loop swung south. Curried rice at Yuraku-cho and Shimbashi could be eaten with unchallenged elbows, and it cost half a dollar more. In a passageway vaulted like a catacomb beneath Ueno Station I saw two men curled up asleep feet to feet as if they had been each other's mirror image, oblivious on little islands of straw matting of the sea, of that endless sea of people who sidestepped and hurried on. Poverty, or perhaps just simplicity that only by comparison acquired shabbiness, isolated these and other individuals, gave them, indeed, that individuality I was seeking as a touchstone to get the measure of what they differed from. Anyone not moving or moving slowly already struck one as different. Late one afternoon in Akihabara, in the wire guts of the city, its feverish electronic ghetto, my attention was caught by a man with a barrow standing in the lamplight on a sidestreet corner. From time to time he threw back his head and wailed a high-pitched chant. After five minutes he moved on. I followed him down the sidestreet, interrupting him in mid-wail to purchase from this itinerant salesman one of the sweet potatoes he was hawking from his barrow against the neon-lit background of a high-tech Akihabara store. In Shimbashi, a day and a more expensive curry later, I found the hawkers' and the high-tech world, depending upon which exit I took, clearly divided by the station underpass; by its west exit, that led into the Sotobori Avenue and a world epitomised a few blocks later by the Sony Building with its musical stairs; and by the exit opening astonishingly to the east into a dense maze of narrow streets swarming with all the flavours, scents, crafts, wares of traditionally authentic Japanese life. But whether north or south, east or west, and at whatever time of the day or night, the loop line encircling the city's heart massproduced a mass image whose authenticity was unquestionable, and unquestionably its own: the intolerably congested circulation of an intolerably overstrained heart.

Out at dawn again, and still seeming to smell of fish, I inspected snub-nosed bullet-trains encased in their Tokyo terminal and looking, indeed, rather like ammunition; more encasement, this time of people, looking spent before the day had even begun, in my favourite rush-hour scenes at Shinjuku. Standing in trains and sharing an enforced physical sameness, I began to feel affection for these people. I was surprised to find them less unfamiliar than I had supposed. I admired the way they could stand in crowds in the refuge of their own quiet, some of them actually asleep. There were schoolchildren, not many, who were fat, but even they had those unobtrusive noses I was beginning to like. It was difficult to imagine a large-nosed nation either willing or able to endure the confinement of this way of life. And when they needed a streamlined service to move more people faster over greater distances, what did they do? Maybe the designers of the bullet-train had just looked in the mirror.

Escaping from yellow-line rush-hour at Ginza, I waited for a few minutes outside a department store. Courtesies were being exchanged inside before the doors had even opened. A man in a dark suit was bowing to half a dozen girls in light-blue uniforms, blue-and-white spotted scarves, cream hats that resembled cakes. Having already negotiated similar cakes on bank employees, hotel reception staff, even – or was it precisely? – on toilet attendants, I had begun to digest my initial astonishment. In unison the girls returned the bow of the man in the dark suit. A minute later they were bowing to me, another collegial hat toppled perilously when I stepped into the elevator. On the way up I listened entranced as the elevator girl made singsong announcements. I didn't know what the announcements were saying, but I understood what they meant, King Customer, the flashing legend read on the faces I saw wherever I went, and the proof of the purchase was in the wrapping, exquisite paper artfully folded ten, twelve, I counted seventeen times over, to convey in unimagined luxury an eraser and two pencils from the premises to the street outside. Not only the purchase. Maybe the cream-hatted staff as well, with all that icing on top, even those bows, I thought, coming out at one exit and back in at another, maybe these bows, more, the artificial flowers in strange places, the pillows for my chopsticks which the curry man had laid on his counter, everywhere the detail of formality that cared, maybe it was all a kind of fantastic wrapping, seventeen-layered, a gigantic cocoon that could give even to emptiness a feeling of being warm.

Back on the familiar Shibuya beat I recognised as my territory now, I looked into my local pachinko outfit, Japanese for pinball parlour, to check how Kim's game was making out. Five o'clock salary men with open collars and goonish eyes, just released from their offices, stood thumbing in the rattle-tattle jam-packed aisles to see if they could beat Kim's machines; perhaps not even that. Just thumbs, everything else switched off. I'm not a pinball enthusiast myself, but as a form of release I consider it civilised; a lot more so, say, than beating someone up. So did Kim, drinking tea and counting money in his office at the back of the premises he owned. How had the ball been rolling today? Pity good, pity bad, mebbe so-so, concluded the Korean, how bout zam ding tea? With just a little help from the GIs who had arrived in his country for an American war he spoke a language of his own making. Wariness he seemed to have learned in Japan, where he'd been living for thirty years. Thirty years seemed a long time for the little he had to say about his host country, and the Korean's stolid face, except for the white scar across his forehead, had nothing to add to little either. I guessed that if Kim ever told me his impressions of this city they might sound different from my own. He stood waving goodbye, framed in the door of his pinball parlour. He didn't look as if he'd seen the inside of any kind of cocoon. He looked like a man they'd forgotten to give the wrapping. Where's the action on Sundays, I asked before I left. What kinda action? Crazy action, I said. Harajuku betcha, said Kim.

At the other end of the park from last week's shrine the area southwest of Harajuku Station to the National Yoyogi Stadium had been closed to traffic and turned into a fantasy land where Japanese youth swarmed in motley tens of thousands to exorcise the past, or maybe just a week of bowing in department stores, at their regular Sunday fashion parade: dance party: festival of freaks. It began with the skateboarders, clean-cut, athletic types demonstrating the standard forward flip, the crouch of the surfer's tube-entry style, the whizzback slalom through a line of Coke bottles, for the benefit of admiring National Stadium girls with clean-cut logos on their T-shirts. It was as good as in San Francisco, but without the adrenalin of hills. Walking a hundred yards and a couple of decades back from fringe sideshow to festival heart, I found myself jostled by memories of the classic rock'n'roll outfits that had been in vogue in the 1950s when I was still at prep school and wearing short trousers. It was all there, skiffle groups and electric guitars, the authentic letter of the Elvis law, from the dagger-pointed shoes to the oiled quiffs that had embalmed a generation, and utterly different in spirit; not an identifiable spirit at all. I wandered through a grotesque allegory, an empty masquerade of time, with a big hole, conspicuously big for me, in the late 1960s and early 1970s. What happened to the flower generation? The long-haired types in soul and sandal whom I had seen hanging out in the coffee shops of Kanda had not sent a delegation here. Predictably perhaps, they had dropped out; and the municipality provided imperishable flowers in any case. Not so the punks. Gently they were here in force, immaculate, irreproachable, with the best horror gear time and money could buy. They didn't need to can music, their radios had it on draught. There was something more than usually disturbing about pink and green hair when one saw it growing on Japanese punks; a distortion with a twist, not of fashion but of race, as unexpected as an Afro dyed blonde. The Harajuku freak show was the Sunday metamorphosis of a crowd I'd already met that week in other uniforms, highschool kids in black cloth with brass buttons, store assistants in skirts and hats, even the cadaverous martyr of curries might have taken a holiday from death to experience a reincarnation here. Wherever that reincarnation was happening, it was happening in a group. Even in fantasy land those groups didn't seem to want to mix. These kids were celebrating life. That was probably universal. They were celebrating it in uniform. That was probably not. And one other thing struck me: where was the Japanese uniform?

That first haphazard, inevitably superficial exploration of Tokyo I undertook while still fresh to its impact drew my attention as much to familiar things that struck me by their absence as to unfamiliar things that I noticed because they were there. And maybe the spiritual dislocation we describe as culture shock is attributable more to this loss of a sense of familiarity than to the assault of too many new impressions.

Architecturally, I decided, Tokyo was an unattractive city, but my judgement was prejudiced more by what the city lacked than by what it offered. I missed the generous avenues, the bordering gardens, parks and squares of the European capitals to which I was accustomed. Later, long after I had graduated from the beginners' class and was able to read books and follow discussions in Japanese, I learned that this dearth of spaces in their cities much exercised Japanese architects too. I also learned why town planning in Japan had traditionally not catered for the European-style square, piazza, plaza, platz. The square is a public institution, where people meet to exchange wares, gossip, political opinions. But according to one of the leading contemporary exponents of Japanese philosophy, the political scientist Maruyama Masao, the concept of public, and hence of public service, public morality, was never formulated in Japanese thought. Slowly that concept has begun to take shape now, new housing estates have developed it architecturally, new townships on the outskirts of Tokyo have even introduced plaza into their names, but public spirit is not something as easily acquired and adapted as technology.

I learned that Japanese society, for all its apparent monolithic cohesiveness, is in reality a delicately interlocking puzzle of many self-sufficient social units. The topography of the country, whose early agrarian communities took shape in the isolation of valleys, may in large part account for the self-sufficient mentality that characterises the enclosed communities of a particular region, a particular school, a particular corporation, even today. Japanese loyalties, being attached to localities and persons rather than to concepts and institutions, are strong and long-lasting. The less engaging aspects of the Japanese sense of belonging to a community I found to be insularity, the complacence of parochialism, and wariness of outsiders.

Only in these terms would I begin to make sense of the features that surprised me, both those that were there and those that were missing, on my first encounter with Tokyo. In a city inhabited by over ten million people I had not come across any evidence of violence, not even seen, apart from the two sleepers at Ueno Station, anyone just resembling a bum; no junkies; not a single handicapped person; and very few old people. These were startling omissions in the life of a great city.

The policemen I had noticed kennelled in a box at a busy junction formed one small, visible part of a crime prevention system that made Tokyo perhaps the safest capital in the world, of which of course I had no inkling. I would find there were thousands of such boxes, not only at busy intersections, all over the city, providing it with a strongly decentralised surveillance system very different from any other country I have visited. The Japanese policeman is on friendly terms with a small locality he knows and which knows him. He is still addressed as mawari-san, literally the Honoured Walker Around. Personified in this way, crime prevention becomes a community responsibility in which local households are able and willing to participate. It becomes everyone's business.

Crime is kept off the streets, but so are the old and the handicapped, the former perhaps simply because they could not physically cope with the ferocious overcrowding of the metropolitan transport system, the latter because they have yet to acquire the place they deserve in public consciousness – a public consciousness that has yet to develop in the Japanese way of thinking generally. Some years ago I was asked to translate a television play, an unusual play in that it had a social message, which addressed exactly this problem. It described a group of young people, all handicapped, who decided to take concerted action, storming Tokyo's streets and stations in wheelchairs in order to draw attention to what they regarded as their exclusion from the benefits of ordinary life. The case they presented showed the reverse side of the coin. Physical blemish is felt as haji, as shame, to be borne in private by the families or communities concerned, not to be allowed to intrude 'outside', i.e. in the public domain.

Just as my very modest purchase in the department store was wrapped with an almost extravagant care because, as a customer of the house, I and my purchase had in some sense briefly become its personal responsibility, so also, I later discovered, does a succession of 'households' and family-style communities 'wrap' its people, providing a cocoon for those that belong throughout the course of their lives. The formality of Japanese society, its occasional coldness and intolerance, only become evident at those invisible demarcation lines between one group of insiders and another.

The concept of wrapping, pronounced tsutsumu in Japanese, is written with a Chinese character representing an Enclosure around Oneself. It has been suggested that the original ideograph portrayed an embryo in a womb; certainly, a sense of womb-like security pervades the warm interiors of Japanese life, where all Japanese will somewhere have their belonging. I came to regret that, as a foreigner, I would never be able to belong. But I still feel it as a privilege, an enrichment of my life, that at least I was given the opportunity to look inside.

In Celebration
Munich

I first went to Munich on a summer exchange visit when I was
fifteen. The master of the house, to which an advertisement
in *The Times* had led me, stood in a smock at an easel, and
was a real painter. His wife wore a style of folk costume with a
brightly coloured apron called a dirndl in which she served the
family rather frequently – at least in my memory – a dish of
potatoes and starchy curds known as quark. For eight hundred
years her ancestors had lived on the same estates in Pomerania.
At the end of the war Pomerania had become a part of Poland,
and it was necessary for her to explain to me why she no longer
had a home. Her son, my exchange partner, had the strange
name of Wedigo and announced when he met me at the station
that he was very fond of 'chess'; to my relief this turned out to
be the way the Germans pronounce jazz.

To a boy, especially a boy from an English boarding-school,
the difference of almost everything here came first as a sensual
thrill of strangeness and excitement. Pines thronged the garden,
the suburbs of Munich still smelled of forest, town houses were
painted pink, yellow and green, men on building sites drank
beer, not tea, and wore short leather trousers and squashed felt
hats that I thought very funny, sausages were white and mustard
was sweet, and the boys and girls who joined us on the terrace
for breakfasts of gherkin, cheese, caviar and smoked eel seemed
as naturally forthcoming as the easy tan of their poolside skins.
Through a hot, headlong, outdoor summer, from which I can
recall hardly a single interior, my hosts accompanied me on

excursions to swim in a nearby gravel pit, to dance under the illuminated chestnut trees of the beer gardens (where, at almost sixteen, the law considered me adult enough to drink) and to hike half an hour away in the foothills of the Alps, which were higher and grander and more exhilarating than any mountains I had ever seen.

I returned every summer, drawn by the flame of deep personal affection for this family and their circle of friends, furthering the éducation sentimentale for which I felt a far greater need than for the academic schooling I received in England. Initially my attachment was not to Munich. That attachment grew almost incidentally from the nucleus of kinship that I felt for the people through whom I first experienced the city. Part of the attachment was a sense of continuity. I had spent a wandering, erratic childhood between boarding-school in England and places, temporarily called home, in the colonies. When I finally settled in Munich at the age of twenty-one it was the first year for as long as I could remember that I experienced the passage of all four seasons one after another in the same place.

The society in which I began my working life as a stage-hand at the Kammerspiele in the Maximilianstrasse was not divided by class as in England but by the regional boundaries between the German states. Nowhere has regional identity remained stronger than in Bavaria, and the German spirit of the federation to which it has belonged politically for a hundred years is less easy to define there. North Germany, and Prussia in particular, has always been seen as the antagonist. At work, I quickly discovered that the High German I had learned from my adopted family was not enough. Without an understanding of their broad dialect, I would be of little use to my colleagues, nor would they accept me as one of their own. Their wariness had nothing to do with the fact that I was a foreigner, let alone an Englishman. It had to do with their fierce pride in maintaining the distinctive Bavarian way of life they saw threatened by the alien culture of the north.

An important element of that way of life, as indeed of Bavaria's capital city, was its surprising lack of formality. My notion of Germany had been largely formed by the textbooks we had used at school, and they conveyed a highly formal image, elaborate and forbidding like the German language. But in a working environment in Munich, not only at the theatre but in all the trades and craft businesses with which I gradually became acquainted, everyone used the informal du (thou), even towards strangers and their superiors at work. The formal Sie was used disapprovingly towards people they considered outsiders. With the influx of companies and their employees to Munich from all over Germany in the course of the past twenty years, the city has become more richly varied and less parochial, but with the decline of du in local conversation it has also become less intimate.

The physical sense of place was also powerfully different; different, for me, from soft rural England, the provincial towns and the spare Gothic cathedral in which I had sung Protestant liturgy for six years of my childhood. Munich was Catholic, baroque, at once sedately conservative and vigorously outgoing; the sharp silhouette of conifer forests and the explosion of the jagged peaks of the Alps, which on days when the warm, dry föhn wind was blowing would loom up suddenly behind the city spires, gave to its surrounding landscape the intense clarity of that most German form of art, the etching. There are some places whose character comes from the proximity of the sea. In Munich, I have always sensed the closeness of the mountains, and with the mountains I associate some of the better qualities of the city's inhabitants: their vitality and exuberance, sometimes rough and uncouth, their dour, caustic sense of humour and the powerfully figurative way in which they can express it, their love of independence and a solidity of character which, it seems, they have also been able to embody in many of their city's buildings.

I used to travel to work through the heart of the city, from the Karlstor to the Maximilianstrasse (a pedestrian zone since the Olympic Games in 1972), by tram. Wiping steamed-up windows on winter mornings, I would catch a glimpse of the ornate Jugendstil façade of the Augustiner premises in the Neuhauserstrasse, the baroque flourish of Vasari's Bürgersaal and the stately friezes fronting the Michaelskirche, the nippled cupolas on the twin towers of the cathedral, the lofty Theatinerkirche opposite the Residenz (the former palace of the Bavarian kings), and felt the privilege of being able to see these buildings not from a tourist's point of view but as familiar landmarks on my daily journey. They were the landmarks of a city whose spirit, I had come to feel, had the intriguing ambiguity of its mixed parentage, a cultural ancestry that brought together the compact, disciplined power of the Germanic north and the harmonious elegance of an Italianate south, which lay, indeed, only two hours away on the other side of the Alps. Perhaps I have 'acquired' Munich because it corresponds to an ambiguity I recognise in myself.

I am one of at least a hundred thousand foreigners, over ten percent of the city's population, who have chosen to make Munich their home. It is a city in which foreigners, particularly artists, appear always to have felt at ease. It is small enough to suggest intimacy, large enough to allow privacy. It is also a city for tourists, for many of whom the city has a moist reputation as the Mecca of Beer. In Bavaria beer is drunk not only by adults but by children, dachshunds and horses. It finds unusual employment as an admixture when giving new copper an old patina, and occasionally for putting out fires. It was beer from the Hofbräuhaus that doused the flames when the opera house caught fire and all the hydrants were frozen one winter night in the last century. I would not dissuade anyone who is intent on it from visiting the Hofbräuhaus, but it has become, alas, the noisy, noxious preserve of tourists. The smoothest beer in town, with a texture something like liquid silk (perhaps attributable to the fact that it is still casked in wooden barrels rather than steel or plastic containers), is to be had at the Nürnberger Bratwurst Glöckl, hard by the cathedral with the nipples. The most stylish beer in town, for my money, is at the Augustiner premises in the Neuhauserstrasse, a late-nineteenth-century building with a spacious, domed interior where admirers of Jugendstil are provided with a feast not only for the belly but for the eyes. Broad-vowelled locals may remind you here that of the two proverbial seasons recorded in the Munich calendar one is for the consumption of beverages indoors, the other for consumption al fresco.

The tourists make their pilgrimage to Munich in early autumn, when the 'Oktoberfest', billed as the Greatest Festival on Earth, confirms the thirsty stereotype on a gigantic scale. In two gorged weeks of eating and drinking last year, six and a half million visitors (many of them children) consumed over five million litres of beer, seven hundred thousand grilled chickens, nearly seven hundred thousand pork sausages, with seventy-five whole roast oxen thrown in for good measure.

But Munich does not have a tourist season. It is a city of perpetual feasts and it drinks all the year round. The winters, crisp and cold, begin to bite in December. When the leaves of the vine turn yellow and red, the courtyard of the Weinstadl in the Burgstrasse, where Mozart lived, is closed, and one moves inside to drink excellent white wine at very reasonable prices in the warm light of its sixteenth-century vaulted interior. Every winter, for as long as I can remember, the same man has sold hot chestnuts and punch at a stall in the Weinstrasse near the town hall. Christmas markets open on the Marienplatz and at the Münchener Freiheit in Schwabing. With the first snow the great white expanse of the park known as the English Garden is criss-crossed by the tracks of skiers who, a few months before, were exercising horses there or bicycling to one of half a dozen beer gardens. The broad avenue extending east from the palace of Nymphenburg, with the bridges over the frozen canal, where skaters and curling-stones ricochet and glide across the rasping ice, brings to life scenes from Breughel.

When the sun moves north across the equator from its winter solstice and the church calendar, appropriating atavistic heathen festivals, marks time between Epiphany and Ash Wednesday with its own Christian feasts, Munich celebrates the season of carnival known as Fasching. In an age when only the threat of AIDS legislates against free sex, when almost no one in this city goes hungry, when the produce of the world can be had out of season from luxury food stores such as Dallmayr or the Viktualienmarkt, the undiminished popularity of carnival with its licensed profligacy is at first sight surprising. Carnival in Cologne and Mainz is a time for funny hats and funny speeches and steady, sedentary drinking. In Munich it is the time of the mask and the dance and the precipitate embrace. In the weeks before the beginning of Lent hundreds of balls, banquets and parties are held all over town by private citizens, associations of butchers, firemen, milliners, journalists, actors, expatriate Serbo-Croats, municipal and state organisations of every description. I have often wondered why a custom that died out in most parts of Europe hundreds of years ago should be so sensually alive here. Perhaps it is because Europe's most ordered and disciplined people (and Catholic to boot) need the catharsis of disorder, anarchy and misrule that only carnival offers.

On Ash Wednesday Fasching ends with fish meals and conclusive hangovers in a triumphant exhaustion of release; but even Lent, supposedly the season of abstinence, has surreptitiously acquired its own festival, the Strong Beer Season known as Starkbierzeit. The monks who gave Munich its name when it was founded in the twelfth century concocted a stupefying dark brown brew to anaesthetise the pangs of fasting they were required to observe between Ash Wednesday and Easter. Nowadays hardly anyone fasts, but tens of thousands, barely recovered from carnival hangovers, flock to the Nockherberg where the Strong Beer Season is ritually opened in March. In more recent years the festival has acquired an intriguing political component, a sort of extended deadline of the fool's licence that traditionally expires at the end of the silly season. Municipal councillors, ministers, the rank-and-file members of the ruling conservative party and its socialist opposition in the Bavarian state parliament assemble in their entirety to receive a public castigation at the hands of a satirist who has been expressly invited to ridicule the follies of the elected representatives of the people. It is the sort of occasion, richly ambiguous in its spirit, that is typical of this Catholic, baroque city.

Bavaria is a deeply conservative, Catholic state, coloured 'raven-black' on the republic's political maps, and it has given the right-wing party a steady sixty percent of the vote for the past thirty years. Regional patriotism with an implicit bias to separatism (exacerbated by a rooted wariness of anything much further north than the Main river), the power of the pulpit in a predominantly rural hinterland, and a scornfully independent and proud spirit that seems, in curious symbiosis, to elevate itself among people living close to mountains, are some of the reasons behind the phenomenal staying power of that baroque figure, locally less politician than prince, the irrepressible Franz Josef Strauss. But with comparable tenacity, if more precarious political margins, the state capital from which he rules has remained a red city.

Munich is the small socialist core of this much larger conservative apple; and there is, in more than a geographical sense, quite a lot of apple about the core. In the 1930s the city nourished the talents of outspoken local humorists such as Weiß Ferdl (whose statue, like that of the other forerunner of the Absurd, Karl Valentin, today stands on the Viktualienmarkt), then allowed them, joking aside, to wither in cooling-off periods in Dachau. The Lach- und Schießgesellschaft in Schwabing's Haimhauserstrasse is one of the best political cabarets in contemporary Germany; and yet, when its leading satirist broadcast a show that highly placed official sources considered detrimental to Bavarian interests, the Bavarian State Television simply went off air and left millions of viewers in the dark.

In the early 1970s I enrolled as a student at the Ludwig-Maximilian University in Schwabing. Schwabing, which can be loosely described as the Latin quarter of Munich, is an invigorating place to live in at any time, and it was particularly so then. It had caught the bright fever that shook Paris in 1968; a bold socialist mayor had begun to implement policies, made possible by the vast expenditures for the Olympic Games, that were changing the face of the city in fundamental ways, and under Willy Brandt the first socialist government since the war had initiated the controversial 'Ostpolitik', which, we felt, would restore even more fundamentally the balance between east and west.

But despite the black berets and hoarse, convoluted exhortations in that least intelligible of languages, the jargon of German sociologists, which filled the cafés of Schwabing's back streets, the évènements of Paris never arrived in Munich. Munich is not good at revolutions. Beer-bellied and even-keeled, it cannot even claim an industrial proletariat – fortunately. Elsewhere, in cities more suited to urban guerilla warfare such as Frankfurt and Berlin, the revolutionaries were fast turning into terrorists whose murderous activities would discredit the political left for the best part of a generation.

But for the most part, Munich's revolutionaries have been artists. Without the patronage of Ludwig II it is doubtful if the late opera cycles of Wagner would ever have been staged. To Kandinsky, Klee, Marc and Macke, Munich offered a harbour that was evidently congenial to their work. The wealth of paintings crucial to the development of early twentieth-century art that hang in the Lenbachhaus and the Neue Pinakothek (both in Schwabing) is an apt reflection of the close association all these artists had with Munich, and in particular with this part of town.

ENCOUNTERS

Goethe stopped off on his way into Italy; Casanova on his way out, fleeing the prison of the Doge in Venice. The Swede Gustavus Adolphus, Napoleon, Hitler, the conquerors of three centuries, came and went. Musicians were born here, like Richard Strauss, found employment, like Orlando di Lasso and Wagner, or did not, like Mozart, although he stayed long enough in town to write *Idomeneo* and conduct its world première in one of the world's finest rococo theatres, still in service, built by his former neighbour, François de Cuvilliés. Einstein went to school here at about the same time that Lenin was secreted in his lodgings in the Kaiserstrasse (Emperor Street, for the record), waiting for the revolutionary flame to ignite. It did ignite, but in the rooms of another Russian expatriate, Kandinsky, who spent two of the most creative decades of his life in Munich. In *The Waste Land* T S Eliot recorded fragments of a conversation, rudely interrupted by the outbreak of the First World War, with an intriguing Lithuanian lady in the court garden of the Residenz. Thomas Mann, an exile from constrictive small-town life in north Germany, made his home in the much more liberal atmosphere that Munich enjoyed until Hitler came to power in the early Thirties.

I remember as a teenager watching plays in a small Schwabing theatre, put on by an obscure troupe under the direction of Rainer Werner Fassbinder, who went on to make the films (for the most part about a Munich milieu with which I was thoroughly familiar) that initiated the New Wave of German cinema. Werner Herzog, a strange, lanky figure with messianic eyes, used to shamble into the auditorium when the lights went up to discuss his film personally with his audience. Wenders, Schlöndorff, von Trotta and, a decade later and with increasing difficulty, the radical film-maker Achternbusch (who was awarded a prize for an iconoclastic film about Christ that was taken away by the Bavarian Minister of Culture on the grounds that the film was heretical); virtually all the architects of the contemporary German film received their grounding in Munich.

All these artists, with the exception of Wagner, were low-budget performers in their Munich days. If Munich in general and Schwabing in particular lack a comparable creative buzz in the 1980s, it is largely because Munich is no longer a low-budget city. Among tourists it has become one of the most popular places to visit in Europe; among Germans it is polled as the town where most businessmen would prefer to work and most people to live. The quality of life, nowadays more than a mere fringe benefit when recruiting quality staff, has attracted a lot of powerful investors to Munich; and it is rapidly becoming the centre of electronics and computer technology in the Federal Republic. In recent years, the price of property has risen annually by as much as twenty or thirty percent. Unsurprisingly, the country's most popular city has also become its most expensive.

Most of the edifices in the glass and steel of the portentous, chilly, post-modern style that I have watched going up in Munich in the last ten years are monuments not to the prestige of the city but to the power of the banks and insurance companies that built them. And these are only the more conspicuous hallmarks of the increasingly sober, matter-of-fact spirit that business and big money have hustled into town. Traditional enclaves, like Schwabing, where low-budget performers managed to inject a lot of life on not much of a living, have been steadily refined out of existence. Kandinsky, were he to expatriate himself from Russia today, could not afford an atelier at the top of a refurbished apartment block in Schwabing, nor is it likely he would want to. It has become yuppie town. A few years ago he might just have squeezed through a door in Haidhausen across the river, where most of his successors have fled, but prices in Haidhausen have since undergone – if that is the word – a similar apotheosis. Not much is left other than the Slaughterhouse Quarter (actually, a lot more attractive than its name suggests), or escape to the country. The city celebrated for its 'quality of life' has begun to undermine the sources of that quality.

ENCOUNTERS

My éducation sentimentale ended long ago. My view of Munich has grown considerably more dry-eyed, but the city has not lost all its magic. It still evokes very personal memories of the exhilaration that overwhelmed me when I first discovered continental Europe. I can think of no street in the world that I would rather walk down on a fine spring morning than the Ludwigstrasse, leading from the old city, via the Siegestor, to the Leopoldstrasse and the heart of contemporary Schwabing. On one of the ten summer days that proverbially grace the city in March, sunshades instantly bloom, people are lounging at sidewalk café tables in last summer's poses as if the intervening winter had been just a dream. There is no theatre in the world where I would rather hear Mozart than in Cuvilliés's rococo masterpiece of the Residenz, and, afterwards, no place where I would be happier to settle down to a glass of wine with friends than in the resonant, chapel-like interior of the Pfälzer Weinprobierstube, the wine-sampling cellar that is also located within the palace premises. In the meantime, though I know I will never want to cultivate closer associations with a steaming plate of lung, folksy popular songs or Franz Josef Strauss, I have overcome my initial dislike of dachshunds, lederhosen, marbled sausage, brass bands and black bread, have learned to live with quark and the no less starchy consistency of the local bureaucracy. For all these contribute something to the ambience of Munich, and they are best met with in the city's own spirit of generous compromise.

THE DECLINE OF GERMANY'S INDUSTRIAL HEARTLAND
The Ruhrgebiet

In a café near the cathedral in Herten hang photographs with views of the town as it used to look around the turn of the century. The black and white pictures show long straight streets with rows of houses built in a severe, functional style, lacking any attempt at ornament and for the most part empty of any sign of human life. Elsewhere people have been brought together for the purpose of some commemorative group photo: worthy citizens with serious, unsmiling faces. A sense of grimness encloses these early records of the town and its inhabitants.

After a week spent wandering through the Ruhrgebiet a hundred years later I am surprised that such images should still seem so familiar. I encounter them with a sense of recognition, they seem in some way more *authentic* than the present I have experienced with my own eyes. It may be the industrial past has been so powerfully documented that it is difficult to escape it. And the industrial present, still in flux, has yet to be enshrined in images that would provide a persuasive substitute.

What strikes a visitor to the Ruhrgebiet today is its astonishing variety – a perception that may surprise people who have only passed through on the motorway. Looping the urban environments of cities such as Essen, Duisburg and Bochum by tram or bus, one passes from modern city centre through heavily built-up areas with predictable smokestack skylines, past steel works and meadows where sheep are grazing, the grimy houses of former mining colonies and modern residential areas with spruce gardens in immediate juxtaposition, experiencing in a small space a sharply differentiated cityscape of striking contrasts, sometimes even evident in changes in the quality of the clothes of people getting on to a bus at stops only half a mile apart.

A town planner in Cologne once told me that decisions as to where to build what were still taken according to the criterion of whether the proposed building would obstruct the inhabitants' views of the cathedral. 'When they see the cathedral they feel at home.' Few landmarks are as distinctive as Cologne's cathedral, but most cities have a landmark of sorts, which local people regard with proprietorial fondness. Travelling through the Ruhrgebiet cities, Duisburg, Essen, Bochum, Dortmund and Gelsenkirchen, I asked local people to point out for me their city's landmark, and was surprised to find that they were usually unable to name one.

This struck me as significant. A city's landmark surely serves as a symbol of its communal identity. Formerly, no doubt, in the times when the pits, slag heaps and machine towers were still visible on the horizon, these were the landmarks that contributed the distinctive characteristics of Ruhrgebiet cities, but since the closure of the pits and the migration of the mining industry to areas north of the river Lippe these characteristics have almost entirely vanished. The enormous changes the Ruhrgebiet has undergone since the last war thus raise the question not merely of buildings and machinery that have become redundant but of redundant people too, the broader issues of civic heritage and people's sense of belonging in the Ruhrgebiet today.

After living for twenty years in Germany I have come to appreciate the distinctive quality of city life as something nourished above all by considerable regional differences. Unsurprisingly, in view of Germany's late emergence as a unified nation, such differences may be more marked than anywhere in Europe. In the Ruhrgebiet, however, it is not so much a culture with a *regional* flavour one encounters as a culture whose distinctive qualities appear to have originated in differences of *class*.

Travelling on a north-south axis from Walsum to Wedau in Duisburg, from Altenessen to Bredeney in Essen, or from Riemke to Stiepel in Bochum, one often has the impression of crossing a border between two quite different countries. To the north lie the pits, the steel works and the dense urban housing areas of the people employed there, to the south the lakes, the green open spaces and the suburban villas of the people who owned and managed the industrial complexes in the north. The location and the appearance of the elements of the cities one sees above ground in fact reflect the distribution of the coal deposits under ground, and perhaps in the wake of this topographically formative factor there has arisen a way of thinking that is crucial to an understanding of the Ruhrgebiet: the mentality of the Revier.

The word Revier means literally 'the locality', but in mining areas it has more earthy connotations of 'home ground', 'one's own turf'. In a bar in Recklinghausen I spent an evening listening to a company rep on the subject of Revier mentality. Although born and bred in Gelsenkirchen, this man had a job which required him to move to Recklinghausen – and apparently that had brought him certain disadvantages. While always welcome when visiting family and friends in Gelsenkirchen, he said, it was difficult to persuade them to come and visit him in Recklinghausen – that was another Revier. Even within Recklinghausen people had a keen sense of what they accepted as home territory. The railway tunnel near the coal mine General Blumenthal constituted an invisible boundary between Recklinghausen north and south, and the inhabitants of the two parts of town liked to keep themselves to themselves on either side of that boundary. In Gelsenkirchen the same divisive Revier spirit still infused a long-standing rivalry between the inhabitants of Gelsenkirchen-Altstadt and Gelsenkirchen-Buer – a civic rivalry so strong that Buer maintained its own town hall as a sign of independence although it had been incorporated in the municipality of Gelsenkirchen for over half a century.

Intrigued, I went along to the town hall of the Buer separatists to find out if all this was true. Did there really exist a rivalry, symbolised by the two town halls with separate administrative competences? The porter at the entrance grinned, mysteriously confiding after a longish pause that the two town halls merely represented the principle of a division of labour; the kind of property division stipulated in marriage contracts, he added in explanation. I was wondering if this occasionally led to confusion when a woman happened to come in to inquire about some insurance matter. The porter told her she'd have to go to Gelsenkirchen for that. The woman said she'd been told to apply to the town hall. Ah, said the porter, but the town hall in Gelsenkirchen, not here in Buer.

Subtle differences like this need not detain a stranger passing through the Ruhrgebiet, but the inhabitants of the Revier nurse fiercely patriotic feelings. *Sumeba Miyako* – 'the capital city is the place where you live'. On my trek across Germany's industrial heartland I was curiously reminded of this Japanese proverb. The less prepossessing a place outwardly is, the more zealously its inhabitants seem to treasure a sense of its specialness.

In Duisburg I listened to an elderly man who lovingly eulogised his native city. He could still remember the days when sidewalks were made of timber and crossing a muddy street in winter could be a hazardous enterprise. Now, how proud he was of his city, remarkably recovered since the war, and in particular the centre with its new pedestrian zone – 'there's something we can show our visitors!' Whether sailing, the theatre or quick access to open country, all the good things in life were available in Duisburg, a city he said he wouldn't exchange for any other in the world. Twenty-one-year-old Hassan, one of a group of Turks I met in the German-Turkish Club (the German half of the equation was conspicuous by its absence on the evening of my visit), told me he had tried moving to Cologne because it would have been more convenient to live where he worked, but after a brief spell of commuting he felt so homesick that he returned to Duisburg, preferring to commute to his job in Cologne instead. 'The people here are more friendly and approachable than in other parts of Germany,' was the guarded verdict of Hassan and his compatriots.

Community solidarity is the legacy of the Ruhrgebiet's mining past, and the Revier mentality is rooted precisely in this strong sense of belonging. Perhaps precisely because the industrial character of their cities was so overwhelming and their outward appearance so often sordid, local people may have cultivated the community spirit and set more store by neighbourly ties more assiduously than elsewhere. Despite my first general impression of an anonymous megapolis that seemed to sprawl on endlessly, when I started to look at it in detail I encountered rather an atmosphere of urban villages.

For example the Dahlhausen housing estate, a former mining community at the Hordeler Heide in Bochum. Built in 1907, the settlement used to house miners and their families who had been employed by Krupp at the Hannover pit until its closure in 1973. Only the glimpse of the pit tower, still standing in the fields surrounding the estate, reminded one of its industrial past. Gardens and tree-lined avenues, the freshly plastered and refurbished beamed cottages in which for the most part retired miners lived, have much more the atmosphere of a rural community than of a suburb only ten minutes from the city centre. The open country so often surrounding the pit heads has created in an industrial landscape those miraculous green reservoirs that make the Ruhrgebiet so difficult to classify.

The impression of the Dahlhausen housing estate as an entity physically set apart from urban Bochum was reinforced by the self-sufficient style of life led by its elderly inhabitants. Notice boards in the street gave evidence of the pedantically detailed attention (the legal status of a bough overhanging a neighbour's garden, for instance), which was accorded community matters. Visiting the community square, I was surprised to find the buildings arranged around a courtyard very much in the manner of farm buildings on a country estate. Here the members of the Dahlhausen community assembled to drink coffee and socialise every afternoon. Many of them had originated from eastern Europe, emigrating to the Ruhrgebiet half a century or more ago in search of work. I was invited in by a hospitable ex-miner who had arrived here from East Prussia in the 1920s. He thought that one reason for the community's vigorous social life was indeed the need for solidarity among people who had shared a common fate as settlers.

But this kind of amor loci, this affection for and loyalty to the Revier, may gradually belong to the ethos of a past generation. At a pit in Essen, long closed down and now converted into a youth centre, I met a retired miner who had once washed off the pit grime in the hall where we now sat drinking beer. Forty years of his life had gone into the pit, and it still drew him back for the weekly dance in the company of his old mates and their wives. He was happy that a use had been found for the old pit buildings, especially one that benefited young people. 'They need a place like this where they can meet and enjoy themselves.'

Not many seemed to be taking advantage of it, however. Most of the visitors were elderly or middle-aged. One of the few young people there was Stefan, a motorcycle freak in heavy punk gear whose parents lived in posh Bredeney, which suggested a solid bourgeois background. Stefan didn't have a job. In fact he had no clear idea of what he wanted to do other than to get out, away from the Ruhrgebiet at all costs.

I came across quite a number of young people like Stefan, who shared his listless, disillusioned view of life. The reason behind this disillusionment was lack of a job, or at least a job with prospects. Many were just turning over as waiters or taxi-drivers. Others hung out in the slot-machine arcades, whose presence everywhere in the Ruhrgebiet was really overwhelming – a sure index of the existence of a significant number of people with a lot of time on their hands. Where middle-aged or older people seemed pleased to encounter someone looking around the Ruhrgebiet simply out of curiosity, young people expressed surprise and even suspicion.

'If I didn't have to I wouldn't live here,' said a girl working in a corner store in a depressing neighbourhood of Duisburg. 'The new face of Essen? It doesn't have one – Essen since the war has remained faceless,' a taxi-driver told me. 'There's nothing worth visiting in Recklinghausen, nothing to see at all,' a young waiter said gloomily on the evening I got into town. These were just some of the typical comments I heard from young people.

If Germany in general is a country where leisure activities sooner or later get arranged in clubs, circles, associations and so on, then the natives of the Ruhrgebiet have a strong claim to be national champions. But on taking a closer look at some of these activities, whose traditions are as old as the Revier itself, I got the impression that here too, as with the entire Ruhrgebiet, tradition and the status quo were in a phase of marked transition, perhaps of erosion.

The huge hall I visited in Dortmund for the annual harvest celebrations of the Associations of Allotment Gardeners was almost entirely empty. The programme of the day's events, stuck on the glass outside, had smudged and trickled illegibly in lines of ink under a ceaseless drizzle of rain. Inside the hall a group of men, wearing straw hats and green aprons embroidered with pears and tomatoes, stood on the stage and lustily gave voice to a song to which the words ran 'Sing a song to make the sun shine . . .' Slowly, in the course of the afternoon, the hall filled up a bit, reaching peak attendance for a performance of singing and dancing by a folklore group from Macedonia. The sun still hadn't come out.

At lunch I sat in the hall canteen with a group of older men, wearing the red, green and white uniform of the house choir of a

Dortmund brewery. They had sung that morning for an audience of thirty-seven people – a meagre turnout, they agreed, but that didn't matter, because they sang for their own pleasure. Many of them were also active in the allotment garden associations. They initiated me into the arcane lore of all the rules and regulations surrounding the institution of the so-called Schrebergarten – a complexity of detail I had never imagined when admiring those neat rows of gardens from a passing train window. Not any old tree was allowed into those allotment gardens, the paths had to run in certain directions, what kind of bushes could be planted and where fruit was allowed to grow – all these things had to be ordered. What was striking about these eager singer-gardeners was the naivety of their enthusiasms. It was unimaginable that Stefan and his contemporaries would share such enthusiasms, and when I brought this matter up they admitted that they had 'certain problems' with the younger generation.

I heard the same complaint from the administrators of the Nienhausen Revierpark, a sort of leisure park with club and sports facilities on the outskirts of Gelsenkirchen, when I went along to take a look at a skat tournament in progress. In the warm, smoke-filled room whose atmosphere seemed familiar from the industrial north of England, the skat players sitting in their shirt-sleeves were all over fifty, and many of them must have been pensioners.

Established during the 1970s, the five Revierparks scattered across the Ruhrgebiet offer a wide range of indoor and outdoor leisure facilities for young and old alike, but it seemed that the younger generation could be brought together for group activities less easily than the older. 'The youngsters nowadays tend more to go their own ways,' said the man in charge at Nienhausen. He told me how the disco evenings he used to arrange here had to be discontinued because of fights and damage done to the premises. One frequent cause of tension was rivalry between Germans and Turks. From a woman working at a youth centre in Duisburg I heard the same complaint. Turkish parents didn't allow their daughters to visit discos, with the result that Turkish and German boys competed for the available German girls, inevitably leading to trouble.

Gradually I began to wonder whether the stereotypical images of Germany's industrial heartland were not in fact obsolete. Nowhere in Germany are the late effects of the war still so palpable. The cities still have something of that ad hoc quality of improvisation typical of an area recovering from a war. The changes in the industrial structure of the Ruhrgebiet – decline of coal and steel and a switch to the service industries – have transformed not only its physical appearance but its character. In Duisburg, Gelsenkirchen and Recklinghausen there are very few pits still in operation, in Essen and Dortmund none at all. Asking passers-by for directions, I often found they had no idea whether pits were still in operation in their neighbourhood at all. Sometimes they gave me the names of pits that had been closed for over a decade.

At the entrance to a pit in Gelsenkirchen some of the miners I saw coming off shift were Turks, and the sign at the gate reading 'Caution! Barrier closes automatically behind you!' was also printed in Turkish. Many of the names on the doors of workers' housing estates around pits and steel mills were Turkish too. In areas of a highly concetrated Turkish population such as Hüttenheim or Bruckhausen, Duisburg, I thought it a significant sign of the times that I came across a derelict church in the same neighbourhood as three mosques. Fast food stores were more likely to be serving kebab than hamburger. By all accounts the Turks are good 'mates', respected by their German colleagues for their hard-working habits. Their traditions are not those of the Ruhrgebiet, however. Their social and religious customs are different. They don't drink alcohol – a difference that goes right to the core of long-established Ruhrgebiet habits. How valid can the ethos of pit mates remain when the percentage of miners in the local working population has drastically dwindled, their predominantly industrial environment has given way to an urban milieu increasingly characterised by the service industries, and when many of the individuals making up their communities are less susceptible to the attractions of pub-and-club than to a life-style prescribed by Islam?

It struck me that while the natives of the Rheinland in cities such as Cologne, Bonn and Düsseldorf subscribed to a common identity for which there existed the generic name of Rheinländer, no such trans-urban nomenclature had been invented to unite the inhabitants of the Ruhrgebiet. The terms of reference of belonging apparently never extended beyond one's native city. The reason seems to me to lie in the parochial instincts of the Revier mentality; the mentality, as it must originally have been, of people brought together from all over Europe under difficult and often hazardous conditions for a specific economic purpose. Naturally their loyalty and sense of identification would lie with their fellow workers, with a class of people rather than with the region in which they had settled as strangers from very different backgrounds.

Now that the pits, slag heaps and steel mills have largely vanished from the landscape, the Ruhrgebiet seems to have lost one identity and not yet found another. Although the legacy of the pit communities is still to some extent there in the neighbourliness of local people, this too is threatened in the changed social environment. Of the men and women who worked the pits and made up those communities one sees almost nothing. Such people, like the coal they used to mine, have become scarce and expensive. The place where one is most likely to encounter them nowadays is in the windows of antique shops: entire mining families, cast in iron as figurines that are fast becoming collectors' items.

PIRATE NIGHT ABOARD THE DELI SARPA
Package Cruising the Aegean on a Turkish Junk

'God save us from the Turks!' exclaims Oscar. His double-barrelled Bavarian oath, vintage seventeenth century, when the infidels were battering at the doors of Christendom, is fired off at the Berliners who wake him when they arrive on board the *Deli Sarpa* at two o'clock in the morning. Oscar may have forgotten where he is. He will be reminded a few hours later when he is woken once again, this time by the wail of muezzin from the minarets along the waterfront of Bodrum harbour, greeting the Islamic dawn.

The German tourists with whom I have gone on a package holiday in Turkey provide a familiar relationship with a new twist. It doesn't take long for some wag to coin the term 'host workers' to describe Mustafa, Mehmet and Yüksel, the crew who will be looking after us for the week we are on board. Even on their own territory we claim privileges. German is spoken as a matter of course, and we pay with our money, not theirs – hard currency in exchange for perishable wares such as suntan, a whiff of adventure, a splash of freedom.

For Tina and Martin, Julia and Peter, acclimatisation to Turkish matters has already begun in Kreuzberg, the Turkish quarter in Berlin. Regular sessions in the solarium have furnished them with a pre-tan indistinguishable from the genuine article acquired under the Aegean sun. Rather more distinguishable from the genuine article is Tina's smattering of Turkish, useful for ordering melon or keeping salt and sugar apart. Peter, in civilian life a fireman, has taken a course in diving, a bonus he hopes to exploit both in submarine sightseeing on vacation and for murky salvage work in his professional life back home, retrieving bodies from the river dividing East and West Berlin. The rest of us set out on our voyage equipped with no more than tanks of sun lotion and a change of swimsuits.

What does one do on a junk for a week? 'The Blue Cruise,' says the brochure of the tour operator, 'takes us along the picturesque coast of the Gulf of Gökova. Whether cruising or lying at anchor in one of the idyllic bays, it's fun and games all the way. Weighing anchor after breakfast, the junk leaves Bodrum Harbour under sail for the German Bay . . .'

German Bay? The first casualty of the ambiguously named Blue Cruise appears to be our captain, Mustafa. Sleep-tousled and still hung over from last night's raki session with our predecessors, Mustafa has taken a course due south rather than due east, reversing our week's itinerary, so that the voyage begins where it was supposed to end. Winds, says Mustafa with the drooping moustache and mournful eyes, winds make voyage better this way round. Sagely we nod our heads at this seafaring explanation. Otherwise we adjust by reading the brochure backwards.

Sitting in the shade of the awning over the aft-deck, Oscar and I consider what other package holidays could be turned upside down like this without the slightest organisational upset, and find it difficult to think of one. This is why we have come. We are *free*, the brochure says. Food and drinks, berths, transport, fun and games – we've got it all aboard the *Deli Sarpa*. True, one has heard reports of the tourist ghettos that have begun to clutter the Turkish coast, the fast money, fast food and fast sex that will brothelise its culture as surely as on the Italian Riviera or the Costa del Sol, but from our vantage point off shore all this ugliness conveniently disappears behind a coastline veiled in pastel-blue mist.

Cap'n Raki is peering at this coast over the bolder outlines of foreground female forms, toasting on the foredeck a yard in front of his nose. Halfway across the mouth of the gulf the *Deli Sarpa* pitches and rolls spectacularly in a heavy swell. Maybe Cap'n has noticed that Stefanie and Linda have placed their hands on their stomachs to keep the upheaval firmly in place, and this is why he orders seaman Mehmet to hoist the sail and stabilise the boat, or maybe Mehmet just does so because this is an adventure item promised us in the brochure. Stabilising the boat in any case seems to have been accomplished by a natural gravitation of human flesh – eight lightweight Berliners fore and two Bavarians aft, beerier and very much heavier men, providing between them the not inconsiderable ballast of a hundred and eighty kilos.

Somewhere on our backward journey (for Day Two read Day Six) the ancient port of Knidos and its famous amphitheatre vanish unvisited in blue coastal mist. There is no indication that the fish and calamares the brochure mentions will surface in our mutton stew, either. With the disappearance of Knidos and calamares the tour operator's frail pretensions that the Blue Cruise is anything other than a hedonistic swim'n'tan outing are dismantled altogether. Oscar and I avail ourselves of the second portions of mutton made available by Stefanie's and Linda's abstinence, Cap'n Raki places on the aft-deck dinner-table a hollowed-out melon illuminated with candles, and admiring the richly star-strewn sky above the isolated inlet where we lie at anchor, we cautiously sip our Welcome Drink (see 'Perks' rubric), an intriguing Turkish beverage that tastes like a concoction of slivovic, madeira and champagne.

The sharing of one's sleeping quarters, normally an arrangement negotiated after previously established intimacy, is the point where the Blue Cruise nights, working backwards, adventurously begin. Below deck there are indeed snug honeymoon cabins for two, but to sleep in them in this climate is to risk death by fairly rapid asphyxiation. Cheek by jowl, then, arranged like herrings, we sleep on the foredeck in the open air. I have room to open my mouth to yawn, but if I close it carelessly it may be with the effect of sinking my teeth into Stefanie's shoulder. Instead I lie on my back and snore, Oscar, too, lies on his back and snores. Very soon we are roughly woken and banished to the aft-deck to join Mustafa and Mehmet in shuddering unison.

After a breakfast of bread and sheep's cheese we weigh anchor and chug leisurely out of Mersincik eastwards along the coast. The bays and inlets along the the Gulf of Gökova, green, turquoise and royal-blue waters of breathtaking clarity that wash an unchanging shoreline of arid, brown, unpeopled hills beneath a sky of unchanging azure serenity, are distinguishable only by their names. Names, dates, a chronology of days passed and places reached, all this ceases to matter. We succumb to the drug that holiday-makers crave – perfect sun-blessed idleness.

Different people have different ideas of laziness, one person's laziness may not suit another. If it is too different it may even interfere with one's own. In such cases one can usually walk away and pursue one's own laziness elsewhere. This is not possible on a junk. The laziness of ten passengers aboard the *Deli Sarpa*, tightly circumscribed in its space, becomes by definition a collective pursuit. And here there is an element of coercion that inevitably generates friction.

In the tour operator's brochure there is no mention of this important item, no footnote specifying Conditions of Laziness. It has informed us about the experience of the Blue Cruise. It has not informed us who we will share that experience with. It has failed to warn us about Linda, for example.

Linda's laziness is a state of such thorough inertia that only medical terminology can handle it. Catalepsy is a word with which Heinz as a medical student should be familiar, and as Linda's boyfriend with the symptoms of total immobility and speechlessness. On Day One still attributable to shyness, on Day Two to seasickness, by Day Three Linda's paralysis has begun to erode the goodwill of her fellow blue cruisers.

The Kreuzberg clique, true Berliners, crack jokes all day long, some of them very funny, but all day long they require an audience other than themselves to laugh at them. To Linda's chagrin they have kidnapped Heinz and tied him to a card game that lasts a week long. Between the card players on board and the book readers, between the drinkers of mineral water and the gin and tonic cronies, the smokers and non-smokers, snorers and non-snorers, activists and passivists in matters entirely trivial, little cracks begin to open up that by the end of the Blue Cruise will have broadened into a continental divide.

But Julia, meanwhile, standing very elegantly on a wind-surfing board of which she is not yet able to raise the sail, is rapidly drifting down coast, and will soon be no more than a small part of a larger blue outline. Peter leads a concerted rescue action to retrieve his wife, and Heinz becomes the hero of the day by sailing back the surf-board singlehanded. Action cements solidarity. Our appetite for marine sports now whetted, we all pile into the *Deli Sarpa*'s dinghy and Cap'n Raki ferries us over to an off-shore island to sample the local snorkling. Getting there and back through choppy waters in the dangerously overloaded dinghy proves to be much more of an excitement than the snorkling itself in this fish-barren sea. Cap'n declines to make the journey twice, leaving Heinz and Peter, today's rescuers, marooned on the island for six hours, until they are themselves ignominiously rescued by the ship's boy Yüksel, the only Moslem on board who is not an alcoholic.

Weighing anchor, we glide for an hour through the blue evening, putting in at a deserted inlet among the Seven Islands. Well, not quite deserted. Several dozen identical yachts already lie there at anchor, all bearing the name *Moody* and a cargo of Australian passengers. *Moody* Australians are building a bonfire on the shore, and throughout the evening will remain engaged in strange dark rites around this bonfire, aboriginal in character, involving lanterns and mutterings and standing in silence on the shore with their backs to the sea for hours on end. Vaguely I conjecture that these activities may have something to do with their country's two-hundredth anniversary celebrations, but the

Berliners have no eyes or ears for any of this – at last they have sighted the Enemy.

The Enemy is a rival group of Berliners on board the *Deli Sarpa*'s sister ship, the *Yabanci*. Unfortunately we cannot engage in piratical manoeuvres such as tacking cunningly in contrary winds, coming broadside and boarding their craft with the aid of grappling hooks, because we are already moored alongside the *Yabanci* and need only stretch out our hands to chink glasses with her passengers. Hostilities will have to wait until Day Five, to which the brochure has assigned Pirate Night. Instead, six of us clamber into the dinghy and haul ourselves along the ship's mooring cable to carry out reconnaissance on land. Oscar has spotted a sign reading BAR, pointing into the wilderness.

The bar turns out to be a shack in the middle of nowhere, run by an old man and an infant, possibly relatives, with a bill of fare comprising six items, all of which are variations of raki. Under these circumstances even Linda is reduced to drinking raki, and after two hours of this bottled hospitality we climb back into the dinghy with more panache than sense of balance. The dinghy has had enough for one day. When too many of us stand up and try to board the *Deli Sarpa* at the same time the dinghy founders and swiftly sinks. Amid hoots of derision from the Enemy on the *Yabanci* and disloyal laughter from our friends on the *Deli Sarpa* we drip back on board for dinner.

Over mutton stew, or is it beef this time, I listen with one ear to malicious accounts of the capsizing of our dinghy from the dry vantage point of those who had sensibly stayed on board, with my other ear I eavesdrop on the conversation of members of a study tour group, whose junk is moored alongside us. Kultur, intones a woman sternly for the tenth time in as many minutes, and the word sounds like a reprimand to her audience, clad in bathing suits, whose attention seems to be wandering. These people, I am sure, have not missed the ancient harbour of Knidos with its well-preserved amphitheatre. On the Blue Cruise, however, even Kulturmenschen are not exempt from adventure. In the middle of the night, dislodged by an attacking swarm of hornets, they wake us with their yelps as they flee in pandemonium to their cabins below deck.

After four seaborne days of sunbathing, swimming, snorkling and abortive surfing we feel ready for an outing on land. In the brochure, activities on land invariably appear under the rubric 'stretching one's seaman's legs', and the site recommended for this on the morning after leaving Sögut is Cleopatra Beach on the eponymous island. It is, or rather was, a wonderfully solitary island with an exquisite sandy beach that probably does not have its peer anywhere along the Gulf of Gökova. For just this reason the island is invaded by hordes of day-trippers who are shuttled over from the mainland by hourly ferries. By eleven o'clock the density of human flesh stretched out on Cleopatra Beach is such that there is little sand to be seen. This is exactly the sort of tourism we blue cruisers embarked to escape, and after only an hour with Cleopatra we seek refuge on our junk.

Cap'n suggests an overland trip to Marmaris instead. Marmaris will be a lot more crowded, of course, but it can offer something irresistible in compensation: shopping. After days of abstinence some of us are suffering withdrawal symptoms.

Our sightseeing in Marmaris, in the ferocious heat of mid-afternoon, is confined to a tour in the cool of the bazaar. Turkish bazaars have changed a bit in the twenty years since I last visited the bazaar of all bazaars in Istanbul. I enter what at first sight appears to be a labyrinth of backstreets where the locals have hung out vast quantities of washing. Hidden behind these garments there are jewellers too, of course, spice, alabaster and carpet merchants, but on the evidence of our purchases local wares are not what tourists want to buy. Tourist bazaars like the one in Marmaris have become cut-price textile markets, Adidas and Lacoste have taken over from Ali and Mohammed, driving from the market place what used to be one of its chief attractions: the fine art of haggling. Between them the Berliners purchase ten pairs of shorts, four sweaters and two leather jackets, and have to pay the asking price. These are the souvenirs of Turkey they will carry back home.

After putting in at the English Harbour we arrive at last in the German Bay. The gala dinner in a waterfront restaurant looks like the leftovers from somebody else's meal. With Peter, the fireman, I share a hookah to smoke out the taste. Its water-cooled fire-precaution principle arouses Peter's professional curiosity. While hookah fumes elicit scorching sensations inside my head, explosive noises are detonating outside it. Turning round to investigate, I see that the owner of the restaurant has done a quick change of costume between the chicken and the melon course. Sweating liberally in boots, pantaloons, braid waistcoat, turban and a gigantic false moustache, he is dancing a Turkish reel and firing pistols through the ceiling of his premises. Ah yes. We had forgotten. Tonight is Pirate Night.

Memories of pirate night are the souvenirs that I shall carry back home: how five of us swam by night across the moondark bay, boarded the *Yabanci* with cunning stealth and executed a perfectly synchronised jump from the sun-deck into the sea, soaking the night-cap drinkers assembled on the aft-deck in a towering wall of spray; how Martin, sharp-tongued Berliner, trod water and parleyed with the injured parties, distracting their attention while more of our marine units removed the ladder hanging from the *Yabanci*'s gunwale and the oars stowed in its dinghy; how a salvo of threats of legal action was fired at us across the water, and how an irate captain of the *Yabanci* came aboard at dawn to demand from the captain of the *Deli Sarpa* that the property of his ship be handed over instantly.

A whiff of adventure, a splash of freedom? Our backward journey aboard the *Deli Sarpa*, ending where it was supposed to begin and beginning where it was supposed to end, has also brought back to us something of childhood. When we reach Bodrum harbour we would like it to begin all over again. For Mustafa and his crew, cleaning up our mess before setting sail again the following day, it does. Package tourists and their pirate nights are becoming the modern scourge of the Turkish coast.

TWO AND A HALF THOUSAND MILES ON THE DANUBE
From Vienna to the Black Sea and Back

Flaubert's ideal of travel was to recline on a divan and have the scenery carried past. A daydreaming conceit? A contemporary of his, the orientalist Fallmerayer, effectively did just that. Instead of crossing the Alps to the Mediterranean and taking ship for the Middle East, which was then the usual journey from Europe, Fallmerayer set out from Regensburg in the summer of 1840 and had the scenery carried past him for over a thousand miles down to the Black Sea; whence easy passage to Constantinople, the Levant and all the spice-laden East. He achieved this considerable journey by the simple expedient of stepping aboard a Danube steamer – an elegant, restful mode of travel, with the deck-chair as an acceptable twentieth-century substitute for the divan, as I find out for myself when I follow his example a hundred and fifty years later.

For me and my fellow passengers, boarding the First Danube Steamship Company's diesel ship *Theodor Körner* in Vienna, the two-week journey down the mighty river is not a passage to a destination. We are absolved of responsibility of having to get somewhere, that tiresome concomitant of travel, because the journey itself is the destination and we are getting somewhere all the time. Somewhere may be in any of the half dozen countries along or through which the Danube flows, often we may not even know we are there because we passed it while we were asleep or busy with our dessert, but never mind. There may be another chance to see it on our way back upstream.

Not many people seem to be aware of the possibility of this floating journey down to the Black Sea. It is still something of a secret. It doesn't surprise me that the majority of passengers I watch being helped aboard are my seniors by two or three decades; being that much older, they have had that much more time to find out. Their company should not deter a younger clientele from embarking on the voyage, who can exercise their eyes, at least, all the way across the Balkans and stretch their legs in five or six countries. Meanwhile I audition for the role of Benjamin on this elderly cruise and feel vigorous just by comparison.

By the evening of the first day we have passed the Austro-Czechoslovakian border, and when I ascend to the upper deck at six o'clock the next morning we are already cruising into the outskirts of Budapest. What better approach to woo this romantic city than by soft dawn light on the river? Clear morning mushrooms slowly over dome, steeple and spire. Chestnut-trees blooming along the banks give way to faded waterfront houses, suspension bridges arch gracefully over the stretch of water between Buda and Pest. With reluctance I go back downstairs to busy myself with coffee, ham and scrambled eggs.

Hungarian immigration officers come on board to stamp our pink visa forms, releasing us via a discreetly guarded gangway straight into a city excursion bus. A charming, rascally gnome of a lady chatters us mischievously through her native city. Budapesh-sh-sh-t. Got it? Fines on anyone who now pronounces it wrong. Over there is the restaurant café Hungaria, sample the interior for the decor, we are warned, not for the service or the cuisine. Café Gerbeaud is the better place to go. A magnificent yellow building, architecturally fine-tuned between a cathedral and a hangar, turns out to be the East Station for train passengers headed west. Capitalist sensibilities are catered for by a detour through a former villa quarter, where handsome houses behind grand gateways, now enclosing embassies, suggest the procession of carriages that must have passed in and out during the days of the Austro-Hungarian empire; whence we are squeezed back into the orthodoxy of today's main socialist avenue, the Road of the Republic, or Népköztárarság, as it is handily called in Hungarian, and inspect the neo-Gothic parliament building, which looks as if London's houses of parliament had regrouped for their photo under the dome of St Paul's.

In the afternoon we are free to graze the streets by ourselves for the kind of sightseeing I most enjoy – buildings plus people plus the texture of light, the three ingredients making up that elusive combination which we label a city's atmosphere. Pursue Budapest's atmosphere along the pedestrian zone of Váci Street, where most people seem to be gathering on this otherwise deserted Saturday afternoon. The light is silting into soft-grained haze, conveniently blurring distinctions between free-market and state economy. Children styled by Benetton brandish hamburgers as they emerge from a dignified nineteenth-century residence appropriated by McDonald's, pavement artists canvass custom with sample portraits of Michail Gorbachev and Charlie Chaplin, VISA and AMEX WELCOME cards lure us into stores expecting us to want to buy the nostalgic wares of a pre-industrial economy – the embroidered blouses of folklore, dolls, hand-painted eggs as Easter decorations. Tentatively I pick out the tourists, otherwise indistinguishable from the locals, by the better quality of their footwear; a distinction that will march right across the Balkans at the end of ubiquitously black-stockinged legs, preferably with high visibility under the puffy hems of mini-skirts.

Who keeps the streets so clean? Street-cleaners with dustpans and brooms, sprucely clad in mocca uniforms suggestive of itinerant chocolate advertisements. Another telling mini-index of the state of the nation, with intriguing developments, as we shall later discover, in Yugoslavia and Rumania. Who makes the streets unclean? The only person I see littering is a tourist dropping a cigarette butt, which the café waiter contemptuously prods with his toe into the gutter.

For a night, a day and another night, bound now for Belgrade, we stay on board and watch the scenery the river carries by. To stand on the open deck of a ship surging down an endlessly unfurling expanse of bright water gives me a feeling almost of immortality. Little arteries of river lead off into mazes, sub-texts of the great Danube novel; reedy swamps willow-wound, sanctuaries of birds enclosed in a green peace that cannot have changed much for thousands of years. Arcadian images of simplicity and peacefulness occasionally flower on the river's banks. A man with a fishing-rod, a child with a dog; a family arranged, as if for their portrait, around a picnic table in front of a house on stilts, waves in slow motion. I do not live in a socialist country in a village on the Danube, but for the inhabitants of its shores I can imagine no allegory of riches more poignant than the passage of our white ship, gliding downstream with its pampered cargo of passengers, so near to them and so far.

A couple making the round trip from Vienna to the Black Sea and back on board the *Theodor Körner* will pay well over five thousand dollars, land excursions and gratuities to the crew included, drinks and souvenir shopping not. This may not be too much to pay for a feeling of immortality, among other things, depending on what the other things and your personal priorities are. The presence of a doctor on board, this side of immortality, is a high priority for our most senior citizen afloat, who will be cruising at ninety next year; and yes, we have high-wire executives among us who appreciate being able to keep in touch via the ship's radio telephone, and a Sicilian lady with a beehive coiffure that may require maintenance in the ship's hairdressing salon to keep it from falling down. The largeish bar serves smallish drinks, in the evening to the accompaniment of a Yamaha Electone with stops for samba and bossanova should senior citizens wish to cut a caper. The air-conditioned cabins are ship-shape, eschewing pretensions to luxury; there is a choice of decks, fore and aft, covered and uncovered, to meet the contingencies of all weathers; and everything around us has a sturdy, shippy feel, with the ambiance less of a floating Palace Hotel than of an amphibious country inn, which is entirely suited to a voyage of discovery. Last but least, in what would be termed the ship's hold if this were a cargo vessel, which the ship's cook sometimes seems to think it is, there is a restaurant where I am fortunate enough to be seated at a window table, providing an often welcome distraction from the food that has escaped on to my plate.

Laws of relativity find application here. With many people in these countries we are passing through I share a concern about food, I do not share food; my concern on board is that I do not like it all that much, their concern on the bank is that they do not have it all that much. Definition of a Balkan: someone who never walks without carrying something containing or which hopes to contain food. In Belgrade there are more such people than there were in Budapest, the street-cleaners still wear uniforms, but the uniforms are very much shabbier; and judging by the capsized shanty towns on the banks, the concrete tenements, cranes and smokestacks of an industrial skyline, so different from elegant Budapest, that we see through the haze over the confluence of the Danube and the Save, there's a lot more street cleaning to do.

Budapest I admired, Belgrade I like. It has the raw vitality of an industrial frontier, a boom town still confident it's going places although it has been destroyed twenty times in its history. Appropriately, then, the first item on our city tour is a war museum, which turns out to be a collection of howitzers and tanks, maybe stranded where they last saw service, in the ruins of a medieval fortress. Through blockish, jumbled hunks of streets that might equally be bits of Athens or Madrid, unmemorable but for commemorative names like Student Square or the Square of the Republic, I get an impression of a functional proletarian-flavoured city whose provisionally assembled buildings have now roosted long enough to claim a casual permanence. Tito's grave is closed Mondays, so we have more time to grope around in the near total darkness of the Serbian Orthodox Cathedral until icons begin to emerge from the walls like photographic negatives developing in solution.

After slivovic, cake, curd cheese and salami, complete with twiddles and twirls of Serbian folk musicians and dancers in intriguing pantaloons, there is just time to sniff the air in a shopping mall near the centre of Old Belgrade; and take back on board warm memories of a dense surge of life, young life, tall, very striking girls with strong proud faces, old men stooping to drink at fountains, the rapt absorption in shop windows that is shown by people who now have money in their pockets for consumer demands by no means yet sated – warm memories and an empty suitcase to cope with a growing pile of trans-Balkan souvenirs.

When I go up on deck at dawn the next morning the Yugoslavian flag is no longer flying from the mast at the bows – in deference, according to the protocol of an international inland waterway, to the fact that although Yugoslavian territory continues along the right bank, on the left we are passing Rumania. Briefly the Danube resembles the Rhine – terraced banks under cultivation, where tidy waterside villages picturesquely nestle. But then out on to a vast lake, actually the backflow from the dam built across the Danube a decade or so ago at the place further downstream known as the Iron Gate: suddenly the ship slides off the great lake into a steep-banked valley resembling a fjord, and here begins what must be one of the most dramatic stretches of riverscape in Europe.

Over the crest of the hills the early morning sun descends in bolted columns, visible shafts spotlighting the water. As we cruise into the fjord, soon as broad as an estuary, passing the spectacular ruins of Gobulac castle that used to be a stronghold of the Turks during centuries of terrorisation of the Balkans, I am reminded of the scenery of Wagnerian opera. Cloud billows out of the mouth of the gorge in sterterous blasts, briefly the sun is a pale luminous disc before vanishing into eerie morning darkness, plumes of delicate mist hover and dissolve over the water. A hundred to a hundred and fifty feet below us lie civilisations that have now been flooded over for ever; fragments of them, excavated and raised above the river's present level, preserve a historical record dating back eight thousand years. Isolated dwellings perch on the steep wooded hills, sparse modern communities on the shore accommodate people whose villages have disappeared. The broad waters of the Upper Kazan narrow and tilt to a bottle-neck horizon where it seems the river must hurl the ship off the edge of the world. Instead, at the narrowest point on the Danube, no more than seventy yards wide, we smoothly negotiate the gorge leading into the Lower Kazan, and descend about a hundred feet via a two-tier lock to a river that hereafter feels different – no longer flowing with memories of its source, but with intimations of its destination at the sea.

But first a detour to the fourth capital city on our cruise – Bucarest, an hour and a half inland over bumpy roads from the dusty, shambling town of Giurgiu, where the ship ties up. The drive across country is a journey into the rural past of half a century ago. In the so-called Corn Chamber of Rumania, a great plain extending treeless beyond the visible horizon, almost everything I see moving on either side of the road is powered by horses, donkeys or human energy. This is a poor country, its themes stark, empty spaces scoured by the wind, a static landscape whose stasis the peasants seem to share; crumpled figures in caps, headscarves, improvised turbans, dense swathes of drab clothes, their movements slow, lost in the emptiness of the vast fields they hoe in little ragged lines. Primitive the irrigation pipes mounted on wheels, archaic the scythes that cut the roadside grass, the plodding Dobbins that pull the carts with the season's first load of hay. More and more dusty villages with cobbled streets, single-storey houses occasionally brightened with ornamental tile façades suggesting an ancient influence of the Middle East, kitchen gardens, gleaning every last inch of soil to raise vegetables, extending to the edge of the road and neat as only proud poverty can be. When we enter the sandy outskirts of Bucarest it is as if we had arrived in another village; a village surprised, after casual extension over the years, to wake up one morning and find itself a city.

The food trail peters out the further we go east. Balkans everywhere are carrying bags, but here the bags are empty and the people are waiting in queues: for meat, milk, vegetables and bread. Bucarest's street-cleaners don't wear uniforms. Some of them are women. I see two wearing skirts and white socks. There is no unemployment in Rumania, says our surly, tip-scrounging guide, adding plaintively: there have to be some advantages.

It is not easy to describe Bucarest. This may be because Bucarest is rather nondescript. Our visit is also very brief. Barely arrived in town, where our view of the sights is obscured by extensive roadworks the guide considerately draws to our attention instead, we are whisked back into the country, recreated in an urban park accommodating the Rural Village Museum. It's certainly worth visiting. But is it a museum? Some of the dwellings look familiar. They are – we saw similar ones, tiles substituted for thatch, on the way here from Giurgiu. Other things also strike me as familiar. At lunch, sipping water from champagne glasses in the splendid ball-room of the Hotel Boulevard, where GBH monograms in stucco at the ceiling corners suggest the abbreviated glory of what must once have been the Grand Boulevard Hotel, it is the villainous smell of minced mutton, reminding me of pungent Egyptian streets. I skip the dessert, sampling instead the local shopping in stores so hollow that I hear the bald echo of my own footsteps. Never mind. This is also an educational journey, after all. Cheerless in itself, Bucarest inspires cheerfulness in those who are about to leave it. This is also the opinion of the captain of the *Theodor Körner*. When we slump back on board he is grinning from ear to ear, knowing how much more we are now going to appreciate his ship.

The sun next morning is a bright red disc, rising as if it were propaganda into the sky over Russia, which occupies the left bank of the river for a while. Desolate reed country as far as the eye can see, inundated by the Danube at high water, indicates that we must be approaching the delta. At Tulcea Rumanian pilots come on board to navigate the final run to the sea. Much larger maritime vessels lie at anchor here, rusty, crane-crammed workhorses that plough across the Black Sea, putting into perspective the size of our passenger ship, which had seemed so large on the river. Three-pronged the Danube now divides to rule the delta: left the river passage to the Russian port of Izmail, right and centre the channels to the Rumanian ports of St Gheorghe and Sulina, which is our destination. En route we pass villages and isolated huts, the dwellings of fishermen-farmers perilously marooned at high water; no roads but sandy tracks; the odd horse and cow, which have to be ferried to and from their pastures; storks' nests on chimneys over wind-warped roofs; and beyond this sparsely populated waterfront belt miles and miles of delta-green fields and the level wilderness of the coastal plain. After Sulina the river banks shrink to a dyke, a strip of rocks fingering slenderly into the expanse of water now spreading out on either side all the way to Istanbul and Jalta beyond the horizon of the Black Sea.

Reluctantly we turn, as if we had forgotten that no river is endless, no voyage for ever, and go twenty-five kilometres back upstream to Crisan, where a motor launch edges alongside to pick us up for the four-hour excursion into the delta – and this is some delta. More than two hundred and fifty species of birds, whose habitat extends over almost six hundred thousand acres of the most compact reed area on the globe, contribute to the world's richest ornithological fauna. We have already sighted colonies of roseate pelicans on the shores of the Black Sea, and on our very first stretch of delta waterway I spot a fantastic variety of birds I have otherwise only seen in aviaries – not only white storks, familiar if increasingly rare, but gaudy kingfishers and elegant grey herons, cormorants, the eastern flossy ibis and the great white egret, who I feel deserves a more fragile name. In the breeding season the birds also deserve a more discreet motor than the one that powers our thunderous boat, at whose approach they start up out of their nests among the reeds with great huffy wingbeats, snatching flight. In the wake of the launch a watery carpet rises and falls, greenwash inhalation and exhalation whispering as if the rush-floor breathed. The further we penetrate the dense vegetation of the swamp, the more our adventure resembles a voyage with Humphrey Bogart on the *African Queen*. Branches entangle the stern, sometimes the foliage along the maze of narrow waterways seems it will close in on our boat entirely. When the engines are cut for a few minutes in the heart of this wildlife sanctuary we hear for the first time its own sound: a stunning chorus of grating, jangling, chattering cries, the bark of frogs, the whine of insects and flies, sounds that seem almost visible, rising all around us to a teeming brawling delta sky.

After the broad canvases of the delta and the downstream voyage, on the way back up to Vienna I collect vignettes postcard-size. I'm surprised by the rich greenness of Bulgaria, the relative prosperity of its towns, the length of its people's sleeves, the wealth of monuments to revolutionary poets who resemble bearded weightlifters. Arcadian, too, but with less sheep in the interior than miles of woolly shore had hitherto led me to suppose. Bulgaria is donkey land, a land of cavalier taxes that lie in ambush at toilet doors, of scowls disguising friendliness, of mutton and moustachios and cacophonous names in Cyrillic script. Easy as pie, however, the vocal passage to Veliko Trnovo, the thirteenth-century former Bulgarian capital beautifully situated in the hills, and nearby Arbanasi with the most astonishing surprise of all, secreted in a rough-tiled, plain-brick shed: the Church of the Nativity of Christ, an exquisite vaulted retreat, cool and dark as a catacomb, actually a gallery of icons, two thousand frescoes covering every inch of its seventeenth-century interior.

High adventure for those that choose to lie on the top deck as we approach Novisad by day, a shining city in the night on the voyage downstream, and the ship's bridge and funnel are hydraulically lowered into the deck to clear the low-slung girders of the Marshal Tito Bridge – only fifteen centimetres' clearance at high water, but no problems today. Hourly the light on the river changes. Mist-grey pastel shades in the morning have broadened into glittering afternoon when we reach the mouth of the Drava River and plough up a green-bordered ribbon of light to the Croatian town of Osijek. Next day I get a bird's-eye view from a four-seater Skyhawk at eight thousand feet: river craft strewn like matchsticks, marvellously mottled browns, greens and tear-shaped purple patterns, lit up beneath the surface of the Drava marshland by reflections of a sun I can see wild herds of stags bounding over. The Kopacki Rit Reserve they inhabit is friendlier, more intimate than the Danube delta. Aboard another launch we glide through blooming fields of rape to visit a colony of thousands of cormorants, nesting on a miraculous tree-island in a lake.

Almost everywhere the scenery of the Danube's shore-countries is a study in flatness, but perhaps nowhere more memorably so than in the Hungarian steppe, the Puszta. In the wake of dust and a strong smell of horse our convoy of carts jolts along rutted tracks to admire a stud farm and the equestrian skills of mounted shepherds in the middle of this emptiness. My dear horses, our guide addresses us, his tongue slipping in the excitement, for already a magnificent rider in black waistcoat and billowing white pantaloons is thundering down on us aboard a surge of five horses. Standing with his feet on the rumps of the two back horses, he drives the three out front with barbarous cries and a fistful of reins – höyar! and they streak off along a horizon so vast that at two hundred yards they seem to be travelling in slow motion.

On this Danube cruise of some four thousand kilometres almost everything seems to travel in slow motion. It is the pace of the river, the pace of the ship, the pace of the Balkans, the pace of the many images carried by: and under their influence it has gradually become the pace of ourselves. For two weeks we have been refugees from the headlong career of western civilisation and acquired an archaic measure of time, time that seeps, like the river itself, from a mysterious, never-ending source. Perhaps things experienced slowly are things that will long be remembered; long after a fog descends on the morning we arrive back in Vienna, drawing a veil over our journey into a part of Europe that still preserves a landscape and a way of life that I thought belonged to the distant past.

THE HAUTE ROUTE
or A Ski Crossing of the Alps in West Switzerland from Saas-Fee to Mont Blanc

There is a pounding at the door. Instantly I surface from a shallow half-sleep. A few seconds to register where I am. Groans, mutters, curses, yawns, converge from the surrounding darkness. Sit up and twist out of two coarse blankets, cross-folded sleeping-bag style, in which I have lain bound like a mummy. A light jigs erratically across the ceiling. Take mine, says Jean-Pierre, slips into his trousers and is gone. I pull the miner's headlamp down on to my forehead, fold the blankets, clamber six feet down from the second-tier bunk to the floor.

Other headlamps go on, shafts of light crisscross in a medley of patterns. I direct mine at the yard of floor-space I had claimed the night before. Take off the pullover, the second pair of socks and second set of long underwear in which I have slept and stow them in the rucksack. Put on touring trousers, anorak. Slip glacier goggles over my wrist. Shoulder rucksack, and clatter downstairs in wooden clogs.

Five twenty a.m. Gas-lamps are burning in the canteen. Bread and steaming bowls of tea stand on bare tables. A dozen men, in various stages of fantastic attire between bed-wear and full touring gear, sit hunched over the tables and eat their breakfast. Jean-Pierre has already eaten, filled his thermos. He takes the headlamp and goes upstairs to pack his kit. Eat and drink fast, burning my mouth. Through the hut window a glimpse of indescribable pre-dawn light. My stomach is coiled like a taut spring. I have seen this light before. I've seen it through the portholes of aeroplanes.

73

Bustle in the corridor leading off the canteen. Already five thirty. Replace clogs in lockers. Lace up inner shoes. Force shoes into refractory touring boots. Loosely clasp. Snap down boot adjustment switch at heel from TOUR to SKI position. Here we go. I follow Jean-Pierre outside.

At just under ten thousand feet the thermometer outside the hut registers minus eight degrees centigrade. To the north, some four thousand feet below us, lies Saas-Fee in western Switzerland, from where Jean-Pierre and I ascended by cable-car the previous afternoon and traversed on skis to the Britannia Hut, starting point of the most challenging tour in the Alps – the Haute Route, or High Level Road, as it was inaptly named by members of the British Alpine Club who attempted the first crossing of the Alpine passes from Chamonix to Zermatt in the summer of 1861. The crossing can be undertaken either way, from west to east, or from east to west, as we are doing. Either way, the route leads through the heart of the Alpine arc between Monte Rosa and Mont Blanc, where most of the peaks soar up to altitudes of over thirteen thousand feet, for a distance of some seventy miles, and across three countries, that it is going to take us a week to cover.

Five forty-five. Day doesn't break here. It unfolds, it rises, spreads like stain, suffusing the sky slowly with blueish and white light. On the edge of the mountain, still on the magic threshold between night and day, we pause for a moment, awestruck by the shadowy dawn splendour of the Alps. Then plunge down into the first slope – whoof!

Frozen snow as hard as asphalt, barking ice, my skis shudder and the tips flutter as we drop a hundred feet and commence the traverse in rutted tracks. I dread these cold starts, my body still stiff, my feet not yet sensitive to the texture of the snow. Jean-Pierre cruises up out of the rut and skates with his valley-wise ski, climbing with the other, to gain height and hence speed, coasting as far as possible up the opposite slope where we take off our skis and slip over them the adhesive furs we will need for the long climb ahead. We begin with a head start of fifty yards over the other skiing parties, who have traversed at a lower point.

I readjust my boots to the TOUR position, i.e. more flexibility for walking, and free the ski bindings at the rear so that they will rise and fall with my heels. A marvellous morning begins to light up the mountains, the sky expands, far beyond and above us, between the Strahlhorn and Rimpfischhorn summits, we see the ridge of the Adler Pass up which we are slowly climbing. Speed is not essential. Perseverance is – a steady, rhythmical pace. Don't raise the skis, says Jean-Pierre, slide them forward, relax the arms. He sets a pace I can follow for two hours without a break.

Halfway up the pass we rest for twenty minutes, sitting on our rucksacks. Other teams passed us long ago and we watch them, ant-like columns, tacking on the slopes beneath the still distant ridge. Out of nowhere mountain jackdaws suddenly wheel and descend, glossy, bold-beaked birds who have come to scavenge food. My guide tosses them bits of rind of a joint of chamois meat – mountain goat, a protected species native to the Alps, a specimen of which he poached and providently salted away in the summer for his winter expeditions. Jean-Pierre's eyes sparkle as he tells the story of the stolen hunt.

Now begins the steeper part of the ascent. When my shoulders start to ache from my twenty-six-pound pack I take deep breaths from the stomach, pumping oxygen into my muscles, until the ache passes. I learn that long, regular inhalations, controlled breathing in and out, is the way to combat bouts of fatigue – the last few hundred feet are murderous nonetheless, and I arrive gasping at the top of the pass, almost twelve and a half thousand feet above sea level. Almost four hours to cover four miles, but also a rise in altitude of over two and a half thousand feet.

It's worth the climb! From the ridge of the Adler Pass we command one of the most majestic views in the Alps. To the north-east the peaks of Fletschhorn, Laquinhorn and Weissmies; to the south, flanking us, the thirteen-thousand-seven-hundred-foot Strahlhorn; still deeper south the massif of Monte Rosa, with the Matterhorn to the southwest, and a sparkling panorama of countless other peaks visible for most of the seventy miles to Mont Blanc in the west. Broad-flanked mountains sprawl, littered with colossal shining glaciers, the peaks seem to shake off gravity and float across a pale blue cyclorama of sky. At a glance, now and never again, we see the week ahead of us in its entirety.

This mighty prospect of the trek ahead reminds me to conserve energy. In the past five days of acclimatisation and training I have already slogged up and skied down two thirteen-thousand-foot mountains; so we pass up the option of labouring on to the summit of the Strahlhorn, take the furs off the skis and at once begin the descent.

The very first stretch is a steeper slope than any on which I have ever been rash enough to set ski – so steep that the snow cannot properly lodge, dribbling menacingly down over a thin frozen layer. I have to see Jean-Pierre slide down broadside for fifty feet, his skis parallel to the slope, to believe that it can be done. So far so good. Then the first turn. Actually not a turn but a jump on a 180 degree axis. Somehow it works. Do it again, and again, and find the slope gradually relaxing its steepness, and thank God when you are down in one piece.

After the torment, the triumph, truly an apotheosis of skiing – no, not skiing, more like flying, swallows swooping and gliding over miles of glacier. Jean-Pierre lays a bright coil of tracks, an imprint spiralling down over ridge, knoll and slope into which I braid my own – ah! with what satisfaction we look back up at the symmetry of our recorded flight, our wreathed tracks, a double helix miles long!

Zermatt in late April sunshine. Lunch at three o'clock in the afternoon. Brightness of afternoon traffic, horse-drawn carts, girls in summer frocks, shadow sharply etched under the deep eaves of tall houses, wordless content, lounging outside on a café terrace, alive, safe, absorbing rich sensations – and at some moment look up, up across the grey-slabbed roofs of the town and see them cold, remote, white. The Alps are still up there. They're waiting for us to come back.

At seven the next morning church bells are ringing. Rise fresh, as if I had never slept in a proper bed before; clean, warm, primed with rolls and coffee, as if these were first experiences too. How little you have to do without to discover what you have. Meanwhile be grateful for having cable-cars. By nine o'clock we are standing at twelve thousand feet, ready to begin the ascent of Mount Breithorn.

We complete the thousand-foot ascent to the summit in eighty minutes. In Zermatt valley dialect JP conveys restrained approval of this improvement on yesterday's performance. Breathless we watch the mad birdmen in parachute harness, perched on skis thrust backwards into the snow at an angle of forty-five degrees, tips pointing to the sky on the edge of the cliff, waiting for a breath of wind to fill the flimsy material spread fanwise on the snow behind them and carry them off the mountain. It does, amazingly.

Avoiding those curled-lip sides of the mountain that suddenly snarl and drop away to nothing, we plummet a conservative line of descent down the very middle of the mountain, striking our first patch of deep snow as we level out on the ridge of the Klein Matterhorn. I wobble a bit here. Jean-Pierre dances through. Traverse deep snow for about a mile, mingle diffidently with those other tourists down a couple of hundred yards of piste, duck under the ropes with the usual warning signs, and plunge into shin-deep powder slopes towards the glacier at the foot of Breithorn. Skis closed, weight equally on both feet, knees bent and kinetic-energy forward drive as you thrust round the pole, always turning on the vertical axis. No compromises here. Wow!

Powder gives way to bruchharsch, ecstasy to chagrin: on a flattish slope I take my first tumble, landing one hundred and ninety pounds of body-and-rucksack painfully on my left elbow. Bruchharsch is patchily frozen pack-snow, the worst of all for skiing; apparently firm surfaces unpredictably give way, anchoring one's skis in what feels like wet concrete. The penalty for the first fall each day is a bottle of wine. JP yesterday, me today. One all.

Lunch on a lone rock in the middle of the glacier, looking up the sheer rock face of Mount Breithorn. No jackdaws descend today. Maybe the birdmen have given them a fright.

And on down, in the blinding midday glare, through heat-rotten snow turned to heavy slush. In a narrow gorge the glacier groans to a halt, protruding a greenish-white tongue like a beast licking hungrily at the valley. Streams, trees; fellow skiers bound, as we are, for Furi, where we take the cable-car to Schwarzsee. The first wisps of cloud sneak into the sky.

At two thirty we set off up the long glacial valley towards the Schönbiel Hut. A tiring half-hour travese, weight balanced on the valley-wise leg all the way, in dehydrating heat, under the west face of the Matterhorn. Summer temperatures prise free frozen rocks, cascading sinister echoes of stone-slides to and fro across the valley. Every time he hears that eerie hollow sound Jean-Pierre stops and looks up at the mountain.

The ordeal of the two-hour slog up to the Schönbiel Hut is forgotten within minutes of arrival. Nursing cans of beer, we sit barefoot on the terrace of our little stony sanctuary and look up at two mighty thirteen-thousand-footers, the Dent d'herens and the Dent Blanche, and the seldom seen west flank of the Matterhorn; not the familiar chiselled mountain but a half-finished product, a gigantic capsized eruption of slabby rock and ice.

Socks, shirts, underwear steam in the late afternoon sun. Men squat outside, mending blistered feet, blistered noses, scorched ear-lobes. A late arrival takes off his skis. Salut! I have come to love that friendly word, the established greeting among the tri-lingual inhabitants of the Alps. Checking the hut register, I find indeed that nearly all my predecessors here are Swiss, German, French or Italian nationals; an enterprising party of Dutchmen; and two lone Americans from California.

While I am leafing through the register, Jean-Pierre has been measuring today's climbing heights and skiing distances. Five miles' climbing, ten miles of skiing, representing a drop in altitude of more than eight thousand feet. Eight to nine hours strapped on our skis. Nothing out of the ordinary for twenty-six-year-old JP, in his fourth season as a professional guide, who has already done the Haute Route six times. A hundred years ago three of his mountaineering ancestors simultaneously plunged to their deaths on Mount Lysskamm. JP himself has broken limbs, fallen off ridges and into the crevasses of glaciers, and passed the occasional night on a mountain without shelter in mid-winter. Born to the high Alps and always a part of them, he doesn't sense their latent hostility, as I do.

For example, when overnight everything is bewilderingly transformed: at six the next morning a light snow is falling and fog has wiped out all trace of the surrounding mountains. Visibility is down to one hundred yards. Jean-Pierre clatters out of the hut in his clogs, cocks his ears, sniffs the air and peers scowling into the fog. He is like an animal tracking a scent. Well? I ask anxiously from the hut door. Na ja, geht schön – it'll do. He thinks the sky is lightening.

At six thirty we set off under the dubious eyes of our fellow skiers, who are reluctant to exchange the snug interior of the hut for this bleak world outside. Another cold start – skiing down to the point where we begin our climb is a bone-rattling descent over snow that feels like corrugated iron. But when we have attached the furs to our skis and begin to climb the fog is gradually lifting. I hear a swishing sound and look back: two men trekking up out of the valley with powerful strides. Not from the hut. From where then?

Salut! Exchanges as the men draw level. They say they have come from Zermatt. Jean-Pierre whistles. When did they start. At four. In fog. In darkness. Ouf! And bound where? Verbier. Ah, says JP. And explains to me that the men are training for the Zermatt-Verbier twenty-four-hour race. If this is how they train, I wonder, what the hell does it look like when they race? Within minutes they're over the crest of the hill and disappear in the mist.

For two hours we climb solidly and see no sign of any other living thing. The mist hovers, opens briefly and closes in again. Spectral silence, broken only by the rasp of fur on ice. I'm too weary to look up beyond the ends of my guide's skis. Only the hypnotic effect of that rhythmical trudge two yards ahead of me is drawing me up the mountain.

At nine o'clock I'm exhausted and beg a rest. Jean-Pierre grudgingly agrees. Ten tortured minutes further to a flatter slope. Collapse. I can feel my ankles bleeding in my boots. How did I ever get into this? I drink half a litre of tea and a litre of glucose-vitamin solution in water, decline mountain goat meat, and instead smoke a cigarette with exquisite pleasure.

Two teams, each of three men roped up, emerge a couple of hundred yards below us. Jean-Pierre grows restive. I can feel his competitive hackles rising. He has recognised the second team as the Italian party from the Schönbiel Hut. I ask him why we aren't roped up like the others. Not strictly necessary in these conditions, he thinks, and roped climbing is more arduous. I find this argument convincing. There's no *hurry*, I tell him, we've plenty of time in hand. JP says nothing. The Italian team draws abreast. – Salut! I finish my cigarette. – The Italians are now way ahead.

And to Jean-Pierre's chagrin we haven't caught them when two hours later, having had to climb for the first time with crampons to ensure a foothold on steep icy slopes, we emerge in sunshine and biting wind on a plateau at twelve thousand feet just beneath the summit of the Tête Blanche. A pre-fab

Portakabin, handily flown in by helicopter as a check-point for the race, provides shelter from the wind when we break for lunch at eleven o'clock.

Sunday, 24 April, a shade before noon. Day three, or mid-point exactly of the Haute Route, in a Portakabin on the Tête Blanche. I celebrate this milestone with an hour's rest, during which I privately divert myself with comparisons between my present situation and the Theatre of the Absurd. Jean-Pierre plays a part, too. Still a wee bit sulky, he is paring his nails in preparation for the high-life he's expecting in Arolla. Hmm.

Ski down over waves of broad-shouldered slopes and again feel buoyant, as if the world were mine. Up here it is. Let it run, calls Jean-Pierre, and goes into a crouch. I slot my skis into the frozen ruts and rocket down behind him on a slope-hanging traverse that seems endless. When our momentum peters out we put the furs on our skis once more and round the steep curve of the mountain, until we reach the Bertol Hut: one of the most intriguing man-made sanctuaries in the Alps.

It perches like an eagle's nest on the top of a pinnacle of rock. Leaving our skis at the bottom, we clamber spirally round the rock face with the aid of hawsers anchored there and ascend iron ladders for twenty or thirty feet, with a sheer drop below. From the octagonal, wood-panelled refectory we enjoy a marvellous panorama in the round. We also enjoy a very potent brew of rum tea, served by a barrel of a man, a lugubrious, sagging French-speaking Swiss, into whose territory we have now passed. I cannot imagine this Falstaffian hut-warden shinning up and down those ladders, and wonder if he has been flown in by helicopter along with the hut's supplies. Not too much rum in mine, thank you, I say to him, having seen the horse-stopping shot of rum he sloshed into Jean-Pierre's tea, and the man grins. He knows I have those ladders in mind.

The run down to Arolla, potentially a fine descent, is a disappointment. In the afternoon sun the snow has curdled and turned to slush it's difficult to negotiate. I do so with extreme caution, because it was in just this kind of snow that I broke both legs fifteen years ago. Even snow-crafty JP comes a cropper here, fortunately with no ill-effects, when he tries to put in some fancy footwork.

So it's Jean-Pierre's purse that furnishes the bottle of wine that night at our delightful hotel-pension in Arolla, which at some six and a half thousand feet must be one of the highest resorts in the Alps. End-of-season guests, two smudged and sun-blasted Rip van Winkle figures descending dazed from the mountains, we have the place almost to ourselves – enormous rooms, each as big as the Schönbiel Hut, cavernous baths, the best view in the dining room and the exclusive attention of a pretty French waitress who may or may not have noticed my companion's fingernails, pared six thousand feet higher with a Swiss Army knife.

Exhausted when I go to bed after the day's five-hour climb and laborious descent, I sleep for nine hours and wake completely refreshed. Alternating huts and hotels every other night, an idea I borrowed from a brochure of the German Alpine Club, smoothes the Haute Route's rougher edges, takes the sting and certainly the stink out of it. I leave that happily to the true mountaineers.

Another monster climbing day begins late, too late, it will transpire, when we miss the first T-bar lift at eight thirty in Arolla and have to wait half an hour for the next. The sun is already blazing from billions of snow-crystal reflectors as we begin our climb with crampons to ease the going up a high gradient. Thereafter the descent is easy, but after two hours we want to seek refuge from the sun when we pause to eat and drink on a plateau in the shade. From here we watch fellow Haute Route travellers crossing from Chamonix, forward bound on the route we already have behind us. In jerky flurries, insect-like figures, they dribble over the crest of the ridge high above us that rises on to the summit of the Pigne d'Arolla; we sense their caution, flailing insect-like with their poles, as they probe the first fifty yards of the descent. How tiny they are! Little toys that run and stop and tumble down! Erratic specks in the gigantic shadow under a shining scimitar, the glittering arched brow of the Pigne d'Arolla – so this is what we are!

Closer down, benefiting from a more friendly perspective, the insects become identifiable human beings with red anoraks and beards and rich Italian voices that sing joyfully as they pass. What elation in their voices! Very small in these mountains, yes, but alive, alive, glee-travellers coasting happily down to Arolla!

Chamonix-bound, we plod up songless. Hot. Thirsty. Footsore. Our turn will come later, when we have reached the ridge and rested in the Vignettes Hut.

At one o'clock we stand on the ridge, looking up at the summit of the Pigne d'Arolla. The sun has already passed the zenith. We face a climb of a further two thousand feet. Jean-Pierre reckons it will take three hours, maybe more. Descent via the western flank, all the way in the afternoon sun, and down over the Glacier du Brenay. Not the best snow conditions at this time of day. How do I feel?

I feel, frankly, less than urgent in my desire to make another summit. My feet are painful, I don't know what my reserves of strength are, and there are still two days to go. I suggest we change our schedule, spend an additional night in the Vignettes, and start on the summit early the next morning. Jean-Pierre says the weather isn't going to hold. I ask him if there is any other alternative. The Glacier d'Otemma to the south, he says, and thereafter a half-hour ascent to the Chanrion Hut. Better, he thinks. So I turn my back on the Pigne d'Arolla, knowing I'm never going to have this chance again.

At the top of the Glacier d'Otemma I have the impression of looking down a billowing white sheet curving away at the edges; a vitrified, wind-inflated sheet, smooth as a convex glass cylinder. Virgin glacier, immaculate and perfectly symmetrical. We cruise down the centre, poling to counter snow-resistance. Gradually the glacier tilts. Tilting with it, we pick up speed. Jean-Pierre gently begins to weave, through his curves I thread my own; skiing inspired by the beauty of this deserted glacier into which we have come as trespassers. We have left not scars, I hope, but adornment, an ephemeral caress that will be extinguished by the next fall of snow.

Tomorrow's snow. Accompanied into a billowing, glacial sleep by the three-part song of Frenchmen from the Basque country, I awake at five in the Chanrion Hut on Tuesday morning and look out of the window. Snow ushered in soft fall, a ceaselessly falling curtain, beyond the fog-shrouded eaves. Jean-Pierre was right about the weather.

We set out at six thirty. Everyone else in the half-empty hut is bound for Arolla, tomorrow – sacredieu! – not in this crazy weather. So we shall be on our own. One of the Frenchmen stands smoking at the door of the hut as we snap shut ski bindings and thread gloved wrists through thongs of poles. Salut!

Through fresh snow we ski blind. On the first slope I fall. Jean-Pierre eschews the obligatory remark about wine bottles; he is busy taking a bearing on his compass. Our direction is southwest to the Fenêtre de Durand; at least, it should be. At the foot of the slope where we take off our skis and put on the furs for the ascent we find just discernible tracks leading up. For half an hour we follow the tracks. Then they vanish, obliterated by an avalanche. JP takes another compass bearing. Beyond fifty yards around us everything is blotted out. We modify our course. My perceptions begin to play strange tricks. Muffled, muffled, audible its surrounding weight, I imagine I am listening to the sound of the mountain. So many different sounds of the mountain on which to tune experienced ears. Yesterday I heard grains of ice scuttling under the hollow snow surface, like coal-dust down a chute, as I climbed to the Chanrion Hut; a spooky sound, suggesting a whole slope in motion. Today I cross a snow-bridge, not perceptible as such until I have already passed and hear it plopping down behind me. Snowfall thins as we rise. Fog thickens.

We climb for two hours. JP consults his altitude meter. We have risen eighteen hundred feet.

Suddenly we feel wind and the fog lifts. Congratulations on your navigation, Jean-Pierre. Framed distinctly by splinters of mountain, the Fenêtre de Durand lies a few hundred yards ahead of us; and beyond it a hole of blue sky, stabbing colour-unaccustomed eyes, auspiciously in the direction of Mont Blanc. A cold wind snatches at us as we reach the ridge, pull the furs off our skis for the last time and ski down to a pool of sunlight where we rest. We have arrived in Italy.

The way down to the place called Glacier, a barely legible speck on the map, is all below the vegetation line. We descend a very narrow, steep gully, sliding with skis broadside, sometimes clutching at branches. Soon the valley is tired of snow, what's left is no longer skiable. So we shoulder our skis and hike the last hour through the woods.

Glacier is a hamlet of ruined stone houses, with one still whole, at the top of the valley. We wash the mud off our skis in a stream and approach an inviting white table on the terrace outside the intact house. Knock on the stable door and elicit a chorus of barks. JP immediately retreats. Ironic – this utterly fearless guide in the mountains shies away from the growl of a village dog.

A stern-faced woman with arms folded, the keeper of the barks, appears and in Italian demands our business. Beer. Taxi. Our needs are the same in all languages. We supply details and a little courtesy in French, which appears to put Glacier's sole inhabitant rather more at her ease, for she unfolds her arms and employs them in expansive gestures of welcome.

In half an hour we are bowling downhill in a battered old cab, from mid-winter to mid-spring. Wild cherry trees ripple fuse of green with cascades of white blossom; forsythia, dullest of shrubs, forges blazes of yellow, almost palpable as heat, in its brief glory of flowering. Ollomont, Valpelline, Aosta. Chestnut trees are bursting bud and putting out little green candles that soon will be blooming white, the grass in the chalet gardens is already long enough for the scythe. I experience this spring more intensely than any before, perhaps, because I am a part of it, having survived the winter and sharing thereafter the same sensations of a resurgence of life.

As the crow flies it is only sixteen miles from Glacier to Entreves on the Italian side of Mont Blanc, but there is no ski passage. It is an aesthetic lapse on the Haute Route, regrettable, but the mountains won't oblige. From the balcony of our hotel in Entreves I look up in the afternoon sun at the longest ridge in the Alps, the toothed, rocky flank of the south face of Mont Blanc. It's the last time I shall see it on this trip.

We made the crossing from Saas-Fee to Mont Blanc, but on our last day we never made the final descent on the far side. Dutifully we took the cable-car up to Pt Helbronner, tramped through a foot of still falling snow on the otherwise sunshine-roof of the cable-car station and peered into the encircling fog, imagining that glorious ten-mile run over the Mer de Glace to Chamonix, withheld after all our endeavours. We consulted bearded local oracles, listened to forecasts in three languages, all predicting the same bad weather for days to come, and acknowledging defeat at last, passed not over the mountain but under it, via the Mont Blanc tunnel.

Thirty to forty percent of the parties that set out on the Haute Route never make it to the end. Skiing weather is as fickle as happiness. It is apparently a quite exceptional circumstance to enjoy fine weather all the way. Readers who want to share the experience by doing it themselves should set out prepared for blizzards, fog and avalanches. Be prepared for the worst. Then, like me, you may be magnificently surprised by the finest skiing adventure of your life.

PEOPLE

THE JAPANESE WITH THE GREEN EYES
Akio Morita, alias Mr Sony

There are no guards at the house in the discreetly affluent neighbourhood in southwest Tokyo, the gates stand open, anyone can walk straight in, and this seems to be a first indication of its owner's availability. Agreeably informal, a woman briefly sticks her head round the front door to suggest that it might be more convenient to get to the swimming pool by way of the back garden. Maple, cherry and pine, rocks scattered with apparent casualness, the seasonal border of white and mauve plants with a startling resemblance to cauliflowers, identify it as a Japanese garden, but not an unduly traditional one. The slim white-haired figure waiting at the entrance to the indoor swimming pool looking out on to this garden appears to share something of its spirit. At a glance he is identifiable as Japanese, of course, but in jeans, jeans jacket and open-collar shirt, sixty-six-year-old Akio Morita, alias Mr Sony, does not give the impression of being unduly traditional either.

Back from a business trip to Canada only the night before, he is still looking a little tired, and Sunday morning has been set aside for relaxation with the family. With the exception of his eldest son, Hideo, they have all wandered down to the pool for a swim – his wife Yoshiko, who has already put in an appearance at the front door, his second son, Masao, his daughter Naoko, and his two granddaughters Eimi and Mano, aged two and one and a half. The high-fidelity laughter of three Sony generations mingles and floats gently across the surface of the water. The chairman's capacity for work is well known, but watching him play with his granddaughter in the pool, his attention entirely absorbed by the wriggling of her little body, one realises it is complemented by a less publicised capacity for relaxation. Is the one perhaps part of the secret of the other?

He climbs out of the pool and into the adjacent jacuzzi. 'You know what I like to do when I'm very tired? To sit in a hot bath and listen to music.' Usually to music. Sometimes to musicians. Some famous conductors have sat with him in his jacuzzi and personally helped him to relax – Karajan, Leonard Bernstein, Zubin Mehta. A jacuzzi is a good place to sit and talk with friends, he says. Mr Jacuzzi turns out to be a friend too. It comes as something of a surprise to learn that there is a Mr Jacuzzi. 'Oh yes. You don't know? But I designed this one myself. Six horsepower. Solid stainless steel.' He pats the rim of the tub affectionately. It is as if the gesture were addressed to Mr Jacuzzi personally.

The jacuzzi, the swimming pool, the roll-on foam cover (patented, of course) to cut down heating costs and humidity, the main living room in which we meet for drinks after a short dip in the bath upstairs, where he seems quite happy to have his picture taken – it soon transpires that not only have large bits of the interior of the twenty-four-room house and many of the things in it all been designed by him, but also the house itself. The house is really an extension of himself, a monument to a lifelong enthusiasm for why things work and how to make them.

The first son and fifteenth-generation heir to a sake brewing business in the prefecture of Nagoya, Akio Morita was born into a wealthy patrician household where the two interests were nourished that would later shape his career. Forced by his father to attend board meetings of the family firm while still a child, he acquired early experience of business. And thanks to the imported phonograph of his mother, who adored classical music, he developed a taste not only for music but for the technology that made sound reproduction possible. Neglecting school work, he pursued his hobby of electronics and had soon built a radio receiver and a phonograph on his own. An uncle who returned to the family home after a four-year stay in Europe brought first-hand experience of life abroad, which also made a deep impression. The Moritas now no longer lived in the little village of Kosugaya but in a modern city, Nagoya, where Akio's father had moved the business in order to liberate it from the constricting atmosphere of old-world rural Japan. He staffed the company with younger, more educated people, and modernised its accounting system. It was in this unusually progressive, liberal atmosphere during the 1930s that the boy who had auspiciously been named Enlightenment grew up.

'So I was being modernised even as a child. Have you ever seen one of these?'

It is an early Edison phonograph, dating from the turn of the century, and presented to him by EMI. With a fond, attentive expression he listens to the scratchy sounds that emerge from the remote past. Then he turns to the convertible Steinway player piano, splendid centrepiece of the living room which his wife has furnished with unobtrusive elegance, adjusts a couple of knobs, inserts a player roll, and the keys begin a ghostly dance, depress, spring back, as they reproduce the notes of a Paderewski minuet. The player roll is one of fifteen hundred, piled up to the ceiling in a corner of the room. The sound quality of the player piano, built in the year that Morita was born, is already infinitely superior to the Edison phonograph. What next?

Next he studied physics at Osaka Imperial University. When war broke out he opted for a long-term commission as a naval officer, because this enabled him to avoid active service and to continue scientific research. He admits he was afraid of bombing and did not want to die, but more importantly the sense of mission, which he had even as a young man, dictated to him that he could serve his country better by staying alive and investing in its future than by making a useless sacrifice for it now. Events would prove him right even before the war was over, for it was during his work with a research group concerned with heat-seeking devices (comparable to the later American Sidewinder missile) that he made the acquaintance of Masaru Ibuka, who in 1946 founded the Tokyo Telecommunications Engineering Corporation, later to be known as Sony.

Sony is the name of the last sound reproduction device that he now demonstrates in his living room. The CD laser system is comparably smaller than the Edison or the Steinway, the fidelity and the volume incomparably greater: the poured ferro-concrete, black-netted ceiling, incorporating two huge cone-shaped woofers, is itself an entire speaker system. A Bach Toccata and Fugue suddenly fill the room with the thunderous resonance of a cathedral, with the Thus Spake Zarathustra of Richard Strauss it seems to take off altogether, suspended in a dimension of pure sound. An outsize screen descends from the ceiling, a video-taped airshow jumps into life, with a terrific stereophonic blast jet planes take off on one side of the room and rocket out of sight on the other. It is the total audio-visual experience, and Mr Sony, handling the controls, is obviously in his element.

The plaque on the door of Room 772 at Sony's corporate headquarters in Gotenyama, not far from where the chairman lives, states simply: A Morita. Simplicity is the style both of the man and the building, and the way up to his office, involving a lot of unexpected turns and bare corridors that seem to lead nowhere, is in some sense a journey through his corporate life. During the forty odd years since the company set up shop here in a delapidated shack the building has undergone constant modifications and extensions, but the nucleus of the original factory is still there, the functionalism of a place designed for making things still flavours the administrative headquarters of the international corporation Sony has since become.

Walking into his office you at once feel yourself surrounded by a warm and engaging personality, even when that personality is otherwise engaged with two or three phone calls simultaneously. There's clutter in the room, conveying a sense of business rather than disorder. Clocks show the time in New York and Europe, a globe stands on one side of the room, on the other side a silver sailing ship in a glass case, presented by the company to its Helmsman and inscribed in Latin 'Progresus in Infinitum'. A letter from Prince Charles, a photo of Morita with Reagan, a document entitled Ordre National: La Légion d'honneur, hang framed on the walls. A set of plastic teeth mounted on feet stand grinning at the chairman across his desk, where at last one discovers something Japanese: the proofs of his book *Made in Japan, Akio Morita and Sony*, which the author is now busy correcting. Significantly, the book has already appeared in America and Britain. It will appear in seventeen languages, among them Japanese.

Made in Japan begins with the atomic bombing of Hiroshima and the lesson it seared indelibly on the young physicist's mind. 'The technology gap it represented was tremendous.' The impact of that lesson can hardly be overstated. Perhaps it generated, in the instant of destruction, the entire energy behind Japan's phenomenal postwar recovery. It certainly accounts for the Japanese obsession with America and with closing the technological gap America represented; a Japanese obsession in general, of which Morita became the personification. In a deeper sense, however, the story of Morita and the making of Sony elaborates a much older theme, which has always preoccupied the inhabitants of the volcanic archipelago so poor in natural resources and so rich in natural disasters: the theme of survival.

Sony founder Masaru Ibuka, whom Morita describes as a genius, was well aware that his tiny company with its handful of young scientists and engineers could not compete with already established companies like Matsushita, Hitachi and Toshiba on their own ground. In order to survive they would have to go out in front, to conceive and design new products ahead of their competitors.

And so they did. From the first tape recorders, solid-state radios and transistorised TV sets in the 1950s on to today's portable stereo player Walkman, the CD player Discman, home video-cassette recorders, the invention of the Trinitron system and of eight millimetre video, the three and a half inch computer floppy disc, the filmless camera Mavica, and so on – many of Sony's products were world firsts, requiring not just the application of existing technologies but investment in basic research. Perhaps the clearest index of that is the Nobel price for physics awarded Leo Esaki in 1973 for his discovery of the diode tunnelling effect, which he made in Sony's research labs when working on the development of the transistor.

It was this obsession with originality of concept and product quality that quickly distinguished the young company from its competitors and made it internationally one of the most famous names in the consumer electronics industry, despite the fact that it was and remains today a relatively junior partner on the Japanese market. With net sales of almost six billion pounds in 1985, Sony ranked only fifth among its Japanese competitors, doing roughly half the volume of business of its closest rival NEC and not much over a quarter of the business of the market leader, Matsushita.

From the very start Ibuka and Morita planned to lead the public with new products rather than to ask what kind of products the public wanted. Sony became the industry's trend-setter or guinea-pig, pioneering new technology that would be taken up by its competitors once it had proved its success on the market. Because of the increasingly short life-cycle of products there was a premium on the speed and efficiency with which Sony could get a new product on to the assembly line. By the time the bigger manufacturers moved in to mop up, the guinea-pig would again be a step ahead with another innovation. It declined to take part in the scramble for the mass market or to manufacture under any label but its own – policies that helped to win Sony its enormous prestige but cut into its profits, and eventually had to be reversed.

Innovative design and high-quality technology were all very well, but what if the public declined to be led, and the hot-shot company failed to sell its products? Immensely proud of their first tape recorder in 1950, Ibuka and Morita were dismayed to find that nobody wanted to buy it. This appears to have been the point at which Morita stepped out of Ibuka's shadow and discovered in himself the astonishing marketing flair that was the essential complement to Ibuka's technological wizardry. Innovator and Communicator – the double bill was launched that would rocket Sony to international business stardom. Morita compares it to the partnership between Fujisawa and Honda, who, like Ibuka, founded his own company, strikingly similar to Sony in its emphasis on creative technology and an unusually high reliance on the export market. Honda has been the other outstanding post-war success story of Japanese industry.

Asked if he regards marketing as a science or an art, Morita doesn't hesitate to call it a science. But he admits to having a sixth sense. For example with the Walkman? 'No. That was through knowing the technology and the market – a purely rational decision.' Marketing is really a form of communication, he says; meaning, in effect, education. Noting the shortage of stenographers in post-war Japan, for example, he took Sony's unwanted tape recorder into the law courts and 'educated' people with regard to its potential applications.

Introducing the tape recorder as a teaching aid in schools and colleges, he took a more devious approach. He formed a bogus company called the Study Group for Audio-visual Education and sent Sony salesmen out, equipped with the bogus company's business cards identifying them as impartial educational advisers, to lecture to school authorities. As mere salesmen plugging a commercial product nobody would have listened to them; and they didn't need to recommend any brand names 'because at that time in Japan we were the sole manufacturers', says Morita, laughing heartily.

He is an astute operator. Sometimes he is a crafty one. Sony's first 'pocketable' radio (the word was also invented by Sony, incidentally), in 1957 the world's smallest, unfortunately had the drawback that it would not actually fit into a standard pocket. Morita's solution was to have special shirts made for the company salesmen, with pockets larger than usual so that they could demonstrate the pocketable principle without embarrassment.

It's a minor incident, but characteristic of his flexibility, which may be one of his greatest strengths. When he went to America in the early 1950s he immediately recognised that the company's original name must be changed because for non-Japanese it was unpronounceable. Looking through a Latin dictionary, he and Ibuka discovered the word sonus, meaning sound. At first they came up with Sonny. Here was an internationally acceptable name, with the one serious disadvantage that it incorporated a word which in Japanese meant 'loss'. By dropping an 'n' the problem was solved, and the name Sony was born. The fact that the company and the brand name had now become identical, effectively halving advertising costs, was a calculated bonus.

Morita's decision to found the Sony America Corporation in order to penetrate the international market (within seven years they were doing half their business abroad) was based on a clear and simple premise: America was the industrial showroom of the world, whatever went on display in that showroom must automatically receive worldwide attention, via American newspapers and magazines and the international diffusion of the English language. Ignoring the trading companies who were the traditional exporters of Japanese goods, he explored local market conditions at the source for himself, acquired first-hand expertise of the American way of business, built up an independent Sony marketing and distribution network, picking up the English language as he went along.

Thus Sony became the first Japanese company with a showroom on Fifth Avenue flying the Japanese flag, the first to put up a sign in Times Square. It was years before the next wave followed. The marketing strategy that Morita had personally pioneered became known in Japan as the Sony Method. His experience in America also groomed him for the role that would take up an increasing amount of his time as he entered the third quarter-century of his life – his role as Japan's unofficial ambassador to the world.

From the back of the conference room at the New Otani Hotel one has an unusual rear view of the heads and shoulders of some of the most powerful men in Japanese business. The main lights have been turned down, here and there a column of cigarette smoke idles up to the ceiling, the atmosphere is relaxed, from the rows of dark-suited bankers and company directors emanates a discreet sense of money and corporate muscle.

The podium at the front is brightly lit. As usual, it is Akio Morita sitting under the spotlights. He has been asked by the Zaikai forum, a select group of businessmen and financiers (membership only by invitation), to come and speak to them about his book. He begins in an informal key, relating how the idea for the book originated from an interview he did for *Playboy* magazine. Blandly he describes the nature of this magazine so that his audience will appreciate why he had difficulty getting a copy of the interview issue through Japanese customs. Laughter. He holds up the English language edition and apologises for the prominence with which he is displayed on the cover; unfortunately Iacocca had already established the precedent. This goes down well too. Thumbnail sketches of other foreign editions follow – the Korean, the Swedish, the very bulky German edition, of which he laconically remarks that either the paper must be thicker or the words longer. The author tour he undertook to promote the book in the United States gives him the pretext to discuss marketing in general terms, and already his theme has acquired the global context enabling him to broach the subject which is the heart of his speech: asset stripping and the Money Game, the deindustrialisation of the world's greatest debtor nation, the weak dollar and the mighty yen, the erratic shifts of exchange rates and the resulting constrictions on the international business climate.

Morita is a natural performer. The ingredients of deft presentation, dry wit, warm conviction, breadth and clarity make it a good speech by any standards. By Japanese standards it is an extraordinary one. Why isn't this man a minister or an ambassador for his country?

Relaxing in the back of his 560 Mercedes, Morita turns down the volume of Joan Sutherland to a level that will tolerate conversation, and says 'I have no interest to enter politics. I'd rather stay in business and influence politics that way. I can call anybody at any time and express my views. As for being an ambassador – the Japanese Foreign Ministry doesn't want any political appointees.'

He picks up the phone, unfortunately not to call Nakasone but to make a rearrangement in his schedule for next week.

How well does he know the Japanese prime minister?

'Well. I was the nakodo, not so much traditional matchmaker as a sort of godfather at his daughter's wedding. I have regular meetings with the Japanese government, official and unofficial. Groups from various ministries get together once a month for dinner, which I often attend.'

The car eases to a halt inside the tunnel entrance to Ark Towers, a new block of super-luxury apartments where Morita has recently established a separate office to handle the increasing volume of his non-Sony business. Notorious for always being in a hurry (his New York staff once presented him with a red fireman's helmet), he covers the distance from parking bay to elevator extremely rapidly, but once he is installed in the apartment on the twenty-third floor he conveys the impression of having all the time in the world. Perhaps this has also been one of the secrets of his success – he is in a hurry *between* places, never *at* them.

Morita's concern for better relations between Japan and the world is not just talk. At a time when trade imbalance was a particularly sore issue he took the unorthodox step of establishing the Sony Trading Corporation, because 'it seemed important to me to import business to Japan. I felt Sony should do something to help. We ran a full page ad in *Time*, encouraging people who wanted to export to Japan to approach us. We had thousands of replies.'

For the same reason he also used his personal influence to help Texas Instruments and General Motors to get established in Japan. 'I was aware of an element of protectionism here, and I believe that business should be two-way.'

The atmosphere in the Ark Towers office is entirely different from Sony headquarters. Here he wears a grey suit, not the maroon-bordered pale beige blouse that is de rigueur on the company premises for all employees from the chairman down. There are no plastic teeth to be found on desks. The furnishings are more sophisticated, less personal, and from the twenty-third floor he commands the very much more extensive view appropriate for a vice-chairman of the mighty Keidanren, the Japan Federation of Economic Organisations, where he wears a second hat as chairman of the Committee on International Industrial Cooperation.

'At one time I didn't think I would want to work for the Keidanren,' he admits, pausing before he continues, choosing his words carefully, 'but as I became aware how insufficiently Japanese business circles were internationally oriented in their thinking, how little understanding they had of associating with the outside world, I began to realise that with my experience I might be able to help. Sometimes I have had difficulties in being fully accepted by Japanese society. I've been called bata-kusai, meaning there is the smell of butter about me that the Japanese traditionally associate with westerners. I disagree. But because I have so many friends – I mean people like George Schultz and Henry Kissinger – I can be a bridge. My role is no longer in technology. It is as an international man, in Japan a rare kind of man. I think there is perhaps no one else who can perform this function of a bridge for the business world in Japan.'

So what does he feel himself to be at heart: international man or Japanese?

Morita smiles. 'I feel I have an international *understanding*. So far as my *nature* is concerned, I feel I am a pure Japanese.'

The laughter arrives in the room before the man. It can be heard moving gustily down the corridor, crossing the threshold a few seconds before the person from whom it originates becomes visible. Akio Morita laughs or employs laughter a great deal, perhaps somewhat more when he is speaking English than when speaking Japanese; often out of spontaneous amusement and a sense of sheer fun, sometimes as a vanguard to facilitate the acceptance of his opinions, occasionally as a distraction when he wants to sneak past without saying anything much at all. Laughter is the most conspicuous element in the Sony chairman's always very palpable audio-visual presence.

At the moment the visual element is in the foreground. He has come to have his picture taken. He is standing against a white backdrop in a small lounge in the Sony Building, the company's showroom on the Ginza. There's little room to manoeuvre here. His aides stay in the background. He's on his own. Lights take the shadows out of his face. The focus narrows. Obliging as ever, he makes himself available for a last inspection, this time a closer and more intimate one.

It reveals something unexpected. His understanding may be international, his nature Japanese, but his eyes are cosmic green. Not a Japanese eye colour at all. Does he know of anything in his ancestry that might account for this peculiarity of his genes?

Maybe, maybe. Four or five generations back a woman from Osaka brought new blood into the family. On her side maybe, even further back. Portuguese blood. Who knows?

He presents his face in profile, betraying a toughness and determination around the thrust of his jaw that escape attention when he faces one head on. Which is his better side, someone asks. It depends who's looking, he replies with a laugh. Banter accompanies each change of pose. I'm worried, he says, resting his head on his hands; or: maybe this will give me some crafty idea, as his eyes narrow with the adjustment of a smile. Good picture, he announces, satisfied with the solemn expression he's achieved, I'd like an enlargement for my funeral, please. And five minutes into the session, ruefully plaintive: how about my fee?

But it's not money that has been the motivation in his life. What has? Frankly, I don't know, he says, and after a longish pause he adds that as a businessman he used to feel responsible for his people, now he is moved by a concern for better relations between Japan and the world. Have there been any firm beliefs that have guided him in his life? At bottom his beliefs are Confucian, he thinks, which he probably acquired unconsciously: work hard, be honest, respect your elders. Discipline in Japan is not what it used to be. His father once ducked him in a pond and tied him to a tree, although he can't remember what for. Morita roars with laughter. Has he ever had any doubts about himself? Practically never. What would he like to have had more of in life? Time. Given another incarnation, can he imagine a different life for himself? No, he answers promptly, but his wife can. She says that if she were born again she would like to be a man with a wife like herself. Hilarity again disrupts the portrait session, and an aide steps forward with a comb to discipline his unruly hair, which displays an intriguing tendency to stand up on the chairman's head in moments of excitement.

Now that the subject of his wife has been raised, one other question – please, of course! – has she been something of a power behind the Morita throne? Not behind, no: maybe better to say *in front*. Oh really? Well, she's rather an outspoken woman, very active, both as a hostess inside the house and as his representative outside it. Without her assistance, especially during the years when they lived in New York, he would never have acquired the number of friends he has. He encourages young Japanese women to follow her example, because modern customs require the wife to step more into the foreground. Did he and his wife have an arranged marriage? Yes, but that's a secret. Does he regard any aspects of his life as old-fashioned? No, and that's not a secret.

Any secrets in his dreams? What does he dream about at night? He doesn't remember his dreams – only thing he's sure of is that he doesn't have nightmares. Not even, for example, about Sony's consolidated results for 1986, which show a drop in net income of over forty percent? The chairman regards this as a short-term problem. What can you expect, he asks, when the value of the yen against the dollar has appreciated during the same period by roughly the same percentage? In the long term he feels confident. What does he regard as his greatest personal asset? Optimism, says Morita, I always look on the bright side of things.

This is manifestly true. Remarkably, for a man who is as frank in his criticisms as he is generous with his praise, in the three hundred pages of his book Morita voices not a single doubt about the potential risks of modern technology (characteristically, what he enjoys about James Bond movies is not the glamour of Connery or Moore but their glamorous technology), not a single criticism of Sony, and only one conspicuous admission of a personal error of judgement: his premature decision to withdraw from the calculator market, resulting in a neglect of exactly the in-house digital technology that Sony was increasingly going to need in the future. What other mistakes has he made?

At the back of the room the PR man audibly begins to fidget. He is not too happy about even this one admission, any more will make his job not worth having. But the chairman's hair remains firmly in place.

'No comment,' he says for the first time this week.

He declines to make any predictions about DAT either, Sony's new Digital Audio Tape system. 'I can't say anything. This is a sensitive subject.' It is indeed. Although not available on the market until later this year [1987], DAT is already giving the rest of the sound reproduction industry a headache.

Sometimes they are distinct, sometimes they overlap, Akio Morita the internationalist and Akio Morita the company man, but in the end it is the chairman of Sony, loyal to his principle that the most important thing in management is to maintain a healthy relationship with one's employees and to create a family-like feeling, who has the last word. Does it sound vaguely familiar? His nature, as he says, is pure Japanese. One can only look forward to meeting more who also have Morita's understanding.

THE CHAIR MAN
Rolf Fehlbaum and his Museum

'I think of them as almost human. For me a chair is a living thing. It has legs, arms, a seat and a back. One can be on as intimate terms with one's chair as with one's wife, and after years still not know its name.'

Rolf Fehlbaum moves forward to make his point, and the Charles Eames on which he is sitting inclines with him, as if nodding in agreement.

'That's the main reason for starting up this museum: to cultivate an awareness of chairs.'

The chairman of Vitra Limited has already succeeded in doing this within five minutes of arrival at his factory in Weil am Rhein on the Swiss–German border, where eight hundred chairs are manufactured daily. His invitation to take a seat imposes an altogether new awareness of a need for delicacy and tact. Charles Eames responds buoyantly when sat on, but in rejecting closer acquaintance with the Nelson, Bellini and Panton chairs that also stand there mutely offering their services, has one inadvertently hurt something's feelings?

Rolf Fehlbaum says his childhood is innocent of seminal chair influences. Until he began to manufacture them in the 1950s, chairs had made considerably less impact on his life than he on theirs. But when he began to realise how many years it could take for a chair to evolve from an idea in a designer's head through all the prototypes and trial production runs to the finished article, his chairs impressed on him the very human feeling that life was hurrying by and there was not enough to show for it. He started keeping those intermediate bits of chair that nobody would ever sit on, at first Vitra's own and then other designers', to document their entire life cycles. In the course of a quarter of a century he collected the twelve hundred chairs on display in the Vitra Design Museum that has just opened, the largest museum of its kind in the world.

In a rural landscape lined with fruit trees, at the edge of the factory premises stands a gleaming white object that looks as if it has just landed from outer space. A splash of cubes, ramps and capsized towers, like overflow ice breaking up under some extraordinary pressure of torsion, erupts and contracts, arrested in a seemingly arbitrary instant of chaos.

Frank Gehry's museum is such a stunning piece of architecture that one wonders if it will steal the show from the chair collection for which it is the showcase. Happily stunned, the chairman climbs out of his endearingly battered old car and walks round the building that has cost him almost a million pounds. One could walk round it all day long, trying to figure out how it works, and still find no beginning or end. Does the chairman regard it as his monument, as a sort of Fehlbaum's Folly?

'Oh no! How awful!' He is aghast at the thought of merely personal motives encroaching on a project he has undertaken with such idealism.

'We all seek to preserve the things we love and that matter to us. I envisaged the museum as not just for Sundays, not as some special place apart, but in an everyday place beside my factory, which the people who worked there could visit at any time. Design is culture, and culture is not just on Sundays, it's part of our everyday lives. The principle behind Frank Gehry's museum, with its apparently arbitrary placing of towers, window wells and skylights, is to use the incidence of natural light as fully as possible. He has created an enclosure for soft, warm light, and for our sense of wellbeing there is nothing more important than that.'

Rolf Fehlbaum thinks that chairs, like buildings, create energy fields that are felt as positive or negative according to the materials of which they are made and to the way in which they structure space. Basically we are well disposed to chairs 'because they are crutches, relieving us of some of the force of gravity with which we are always encumbered.' A chair museum as user friendly and as agreeably informal in its atmosphere as the Vitra Design Museum will accordingly have to answer a question close to the hearts of all gravity-encumbered museum visitors in general and visitors to this one in particular: are these chairs just for looking at or is one allowed to sit on them?

Yes, sit on me, are the chairman's natural instincts, but at this point his schedule intervenes and he defers the question to his curator. A very large, soft-mannered man, the curator is waiting at the entrance to the warehouse to show the hoard of treasures that for lack of space cannot be on permanent display in the museum.

'Chairs of historic design interest,' explains Alexander von Vegesack, 'such as this 1928 chaise longue by Le Corbusier, for example, or these tubular steel chairs by the likes of Marcel Breuer and Mies van der Rohe – *that*? that's Eero Saarinen's womb chair, and *this* one incidentally is the first TWA transatlantic flight seat from the 1930s – nowadays fetch astronomical prices. One just doesn't sit on chairs worth fifty or seventy thousand pounds. And there are chairs by modern designers like Stefan Wewerka not even intended for sitting on at all. There's one over there, in a sealed glass case, so you can't actually get at it, you see. So what we are thinking is that we will have reproductions of famous chairs made for our museum visitors to sit on.'

It turns out that the curator is in charge of a lot of chairs that used to be in his own collection. Most of them were bought by a museum in Vienna, a couple of hundred have found a home here. He admits that he avoided sitting on his chairs, and with an apologetic gesture at his bulk indicates what might have happened if he had tried.

ENCOUNTERS

Scholarly, selflessly devoted to chairs (at home in France he makes robuster, more serviceable chairs himself), Alexander von Vegesack has been the guiding spirit behind his sponsor's wayward collecting passion, channelling it along the lines that will make the museum a unique institution, not merely as a freakish collection of chairs, but as a record of industrial furniture design and thus of broader social history. It begins with Thonet's first industrial chair of 1836 and other bentwood models up to 1866, illustrates mass-produced bentwood chairs between 1860 and 1890, takes in Viennese architectural designs around the turn of the century before passing on to the stern functionalism of the Bauhaus period and the softer, curving lines of Scandinavian offshoots such as Alvar Aalto's laminated wood furniture, and incorporates all the classic models of a century of European and American design right up to the present day. Almost a quarter of the collection is devoted to Charles Eames and the complete documentation of his designs, including all the prototypes and first-run pieces.

Can the curator imagine the world's first chair?

'From the moment homo erectus got to his feet he probably felt the urge to sit down. I don't know, perhaps on a rock or something. But the *Ur*-chair, as we know it today, was undoubtedly the throne, and that dates back at least as far as the Egyptians. The throne is the seat of power, a status symbol.'

Today's equivalent would be the executive chair. Office chairs are an index of the power of the person sitting on them and are allocated for just that reason in models of diminishing splendour from the top floor down. But however intriguing the chair's past, what the curator has to say about its future really makes one sit up.

'People sit at their work for an estimated eighty thousand hours in the course of a working lifetime. And seventy percent of all sedentary workers suffer from muscle atrophy and bone damage. For the future I predict self-activating chairs that will regulate the sitter's posture. We are going to need dynamic chairs, enforcing activity on us while we sit – that leg up a bit, that one down, stimuli to the spinal column to straighten up and what have you, when the chair thinks we've been sitting too long in the same position. One day we'll spend as much on chairs as we now do on cars. Human beings were not built to sit for the long hours we've become accustomed to, and at the rate our bodies are deteriorating our grandchildren will no longer be able to.'

We must sit for what we're worth while we still can. Our chairs are already being consigned to museums.

THE PENCIL MAKERS
Faber-Castell

I t very nearly meant the end of a business that had been owned and run by the same family for well over two hundred years. 'Five sons and no heir!' mocked a newspaper headline at the time.

As with royalty, continuity of tradition is an asset but also a potential weakness in the running of a family enterprise. In 1975 Count Roland von Faber-Castell, who had managed the world-famous pencil company for almost half a century, was an old and sick man. Somebody had to take over. It was not a problem of there being no heir apparent, but of there being, apparently, too many. The old count vacillated. By his first two marriages he had ten children, and the choice of a successor was further complicated by a third marriage late in life to a woman who was never fully accepted by her stepchildren. They knew of the ambitions she had for her own son, whom she had brought into the marriage.

The first succession crisis occurred at the end of the last century. Lothar Faber, the grand old man of the company, outlived both his son and his grandsons. His despotic style of management had long ago alienated his brothers, who had founded rival firms that posed a serious threat to the company, so at the sad end of his successful life he found himself left with no alternative but to nominate his granddaughter Ottilie as his successor. Ottilie married into one of the oldest Bavarian noble families, and under the double-barrelled name Faber-Castell the firm survived two disastrous world wars, the confiscation of overseas assets and the potentially hazardous leadership of aristocrats with a background as cavalry officers and landowners but not as modern business managers.

Thus Faber-Castell was not in good shape in 1975 at the time of the succession crisis. The management was old-fashioned. It had become too reliant on traditional products. It lacked a clear direction in product areas where one could expect growth. 'I had unpleasant visions of the pencil market being just washed away,' recalled Count Anton, the third of Roland's five sons.

When his father fell ill he was enjoying his independent life as an investment banker in New York. Conscious of the burden of the family tradition in Europe, he had wanted to carve out a career for himself, to make it on his own. 'It's a handicap when you can only look back at a great past. People feel sorry for you.' So it was with some reluctance that he responded to the call of family duty and returned to the small provincial German town of Stein, outside Nuremberg.

Investment banking in the United States had taught him at first hand that family businesses could survive only if they had competent professionals in charge. It had also taught him how susceptible they were to intrigue among family members. He agreed to take over from his father on condition that the responsibility would be his and his alone. The family submitted. At the age of thirty-seven he became sole managing partner of the Faber-Castell group of companies.

'My father decided I should be his heir, although I wasn't the oldest son and didn't much relish taking on the job,' Count Anton says. 'Privately I had, and still have, excellent relations with my oldest half-brother, Alexander; but in business we could never have worked together. My advantage over him was my education – broader and more geared to modern business management. We had long talks before I took over. One of us had to do it, if we were to prevent the business from falling apart.

'But I didn't want to find myself sitting on an ejector seat.

That's why I had to insist on having sole control of the company. Most of my brothers and sisters accepted the necessity of that decision – certainly Alexander did. Being a true Castell, an aristocrat, he knew the family rule that one, and only one, takes over – not necessarily the oldest – and that the others must support him.' It was a severe test of family solidarity.

To save the business, sacrifices had to be made. Anton's nine brothers and sisters duly signed legal renouncements, leaving them with no influence in the running of the business, and a minority share of forty-five percent divided equally among them. As the holder of the majority share, with sole control of the company and the right of residence in the family home, Anton emerged from the succession issue as the only absolute winner.

The company he now runs was founded by a carpenter named Caspar Faber in the village of Stein in 1761, two centuries after the first modern lead pencils had begun to be made in England with graphite mined in Cumberland. For three generations the life of the village pencil makers hardly changed. The business employed a dozen or so craftsmen and its products were still carried to market in willow baskets by the master's wife.

But the fourth generation of pencil makers in Stein woke up to the outside world. Lothar Faber, the founder's great-grandson, acquired something none of his predecessors had had – an education. He learned Latin and double-entry book-keeping, was apprenticed to a bank and travelled extensively through Europe. In 1839, when he returned from a three-year stay in Paris to take over the business, he brought home to his slumbering village the ambitions of the new industrial age: he would produce the finest quality pencils in the world and become a millionaire.

He did. Lothar built factories and mechanised pencil production. He improved the quality, exploiting Conté's process of blending graphite powder with clay and water (which remains the basis of pencil manufacture). He broke the monopoly of local dealers by securing his own raw material sources and creating his own markets. He founded foreign subsidiaries in New York, London, Paris, Vienna and St Petersburg: he even acquired from the Tsar himself a concession to a graphite mine in Siberia. The raw material travelled thousands of miles by reindeer across Russia, then by ship and cart to the village where the modest family villa soon made way for an imposing castle in the style of the Italian Renaissance, on a hill overlooking his empire.

By the mid-nineteenth century Faber pencils had become synonymous with outstanding quality and Lothar had established standards that still influence the industry today. He is acknowledged to be the inventor of the hexagonal pencil. He introduced a uniform length and a detailed scale of grades of hardness of the lead. He was one of the first to use posters to promote industrial products, and certainly the first producer of writing materials to mark products with his name. Thus the pencils so highly praised by van Gogh in a letter to van Rappard and the pencil Bismarck used to stop his pipe are identifiable as Faber products.

The self-made man made his million, and more. For his services to industry and industrial design he was given a hereditary peerage by Ludwig II and later became a Councillor to the Bavarian Crown. Lothar von Faber, far ahead of his time, went on to establish banks and insurance companies, workers' educational facilities and welfare schemes, some still operative.

Benign, but with an iron hand, he ruled his pencil empire for fifty-seven years. A lot of water would flow under the bridge in Stein, he confided to his diary, before an heir was born whose achievements would bear comparison with his own.

'He conquered the world with one product. I think it will be very difficult to accomplish something comparable,' says Count Anton, Lothar's great-great-grandson and eighth generation heir. Last year he presided over the 225th anniversary celebrations of a company that is now one of the oldest surviving family businesses in Germany.

The Fabers are dark and have brown eyes, the Castells tend to be blue-eyed and fair. Count Anton is unmistakably a Castell, both in his complexion and his impeccably aristocratic manner. Decency, modesty and kindness, the qualities he names when asked to describe the meaning for him of the phrase noblesse oblige, are the values he considers exemplified by his father. From his mother he learned the values of a critical and intellectually inquiring mind, a spirit of independence and a love of freedom. Perhaps it is from her side, the Sprecher-Bernegg family, one of the oldest in Switzerland, that he inherited his high, Slavic cheekbones; also an artistic streak.

He speaks German with a barely perceptible Swiss accent, a reminder of the many years he lived there. After boarding school in Zuoz he graduated from Zurich University with a law degree, and having completed a two-year traineeship with Faber-Castell he returned to Switzerland to take a course in business management at Imede. For five years thereafter he worked in investment banking, first in London and then in New York, with one of the leading international finance houses in the Eurodollar market. Significantly, he is the first manager of the family business since Lothar to have received a specialist professional training combined with an international approach.

The count decided at the start that he would run the family business as professionally as if it were a corporation. His first step was to establish an advisory board of men of proven business experience. With their assistance he set about restructuring the company internally, pulling in new management from outside.

The product range of five thousand items was halved and unprofitable concerns were closed down. New products, such as computer-aided designs, plotter points, and cosmetics under private label for many of the industry's leading manufacturers were established to compensate for lost markets (the market for slide-rules had virtually disappeared with the arrival of electronic calculators), and the emphasis was shifted from the home to the international market. The count founded a Faber-Castell division in the UK, subsidiaries in the Far East, strengthened business in the US (where he had a minority share in a well-managed, fast-growing affiliate) and expanded production facilities in Brazil, where he has a seventy percent share in the world's largest pencil factory.

'As chief executive I had to learn to delegate, to leave practical details to a chief operating officer, because I lacked the experience. I saw my task as the creation of new concepts, of new product lines, getting the right people together for that. Surrounding yourself with people who complement you – that's the art of management.'

Under his aegis the company began to specialise, expanding in selected market segments. Faber-Castell is a market leader in high-quality wood case pencils, high-priced mechanical pencils, markers, and certain types of technical drawing instruments. It is the world's leading manufacturer of standard wood case pencils, still the mainstay of the business, with an annual production of over a billion.

The headstrong young count failed in his early ambition to turn the company round within two years. He learned that it takes five to ten years to get into a new market and control it. But within a decade the business had approximately doubled.

When the aristocratic Castells did the Fabers the honour of marrying into their successful but socially inferior family they at once set about changing the tone of the place. Lothar's paltry Italian Renaissance castle was not good enough for them. Beside the castle, literally overshadowing it, they built a splendid hundred-room castle in the neo-Romanesque style.

The present count doesn't summon his directors to report to him in the castle as some of his predecessors did but, looking across from the dark-panelled rooms of his office building to the early twentieth-century factory complex dominated by its towering red-brick chimney, one wonders if he feels this kind of family empire to be something of an anachronism.

On the contrary, he says: 'So many concerns today have become anonymous. It's difficult to motivate people working just for shareholders and a board. The sense of belonging to a family that we have here makes it much easier to motivate people. Their families and our family have worked together for generations. Older employees work for me, for me personally. The younger ones don't identify to the same extent, but recently I've noticed a change in their values – they're becoming more conservative.'

He describes his role as 'basically the top salesman of the company', and here the aristocratic family name is definitely a bonus. The count finds his title useful for opening closed doors. Marketing his product means marketing himself. Selling starts when someone says no, he remarks, and it may be just a little bit harder to say no to a count.

The inherited quality of the family Castell reinforced a different obsession with quality, one that Anton shares with the Faber ancestor he most admires. 'Lothar was a master of marketing. He spent a lot of money projecting the quality of his products in the quality of his advertising. Superb. Printed the company name in gold. Had boxes inlaid with blue velvet. Employed high quality people. That's the key today. Stick to quality, establish your niche. For me the challenge will be to transfer the good image of established products to a new and quite different range.'

In the year 2000, he believes, the market for traditional wood case pencils will still be there, though quite a bit smaller. Despite steep growth rates of mechanical pencils in recent years there has been no reduction in the traditional pencil market. The advantage of the graphite pencil over all other manual markers is that its traces are erasable. In developing countries it remains an important education aid – it doesn't dry out, it's long-lasting, and it has no mechanism to go wrong. For artists it will probably remain irreplaceable.

But his company has not played the pioneering role in this century that it played in the past. With a few exceptions such as Bic's ball-point pen and Faber-Castell's own automatic pencil, almost every major innovation in writing implement technology since the war has come from Japan: the mechanical pencil, the felt-tip pen and, all important, new ink technologies.

If one judges the count's priorities by his vocabulary, technology is not one of them. Quality, design, packaging, visibility, image – these are the words that recur again and again. Exclusive. Limited edition. Like the stylish fineliners and fountain pens he produces under the Porsche label. Or the cosmetic products he is considering marketing under his own label as a sideline to the already established business as a supplier to international cosmetic companies. He is interested in the value added to a product by the fashion element. These are the ideas he likes to try out on stylish people like Karl Lagerfeld. Probably most persuasively. The count is himself a very stylish man.

He lives alone in an exquisite country house fifteen minutes by Porsche from the office, factory, and now deserted castles in Stein. Surrounded by cottages accommodating gardener, forester, chauffeur and domestic staff, it has more than a little of the air of a manor house; and its master, at home, just a little of the air of a contemporary lord of the manor. His privacy is guaranteed. The three thousand hectares of forest enclosing his quiet belong to the count, or, more precisely, to his family,

Friends occasionally come to stay, his brother and sisters are frequent visitors. He doesn't have much of a social life. The company occupies most of his waking hours, and he has a score of other duties besides. He is chairman of the Albrecht Dürer Society, the association of the German pencil industry and of an industrial museum foundation; a board member of insurance companies and a trade advisory council; a patron of the church and the arts, and supporter of a range of welfare activities. He has his estates to tend and owns a restaurant nearby.

Does he consider himself rich? 'I guess I am. But the things I own are things I can't sell.'

He is an intense, serious person, warm once one has penetrated his reserve. He admits he has taken a long time to learn to come out of his shell. He is still learning how to relax. Sport helps: the former Swiss rowing champion runs through the forest with his dogs and likes to play tennis, when he can find a partner.

Since the divorce from his wife Carla he has become solitary in his private life. A Faber-Castell heir is there, his seven-year-old son Charles Alexander, but this doesn't add up to the kind of family life that he and his employees had hoped for at the hub of the family business.

Local gossip doesn't worry him, his own sense of responsibility for the family does. 'One needs somebody to hold the family together, a woman. If something were to happen to me, I don't know how the family would carry on. Of course I hope that some day my son will step into my shoes, but who can say now if he'll want to? It's dangerous, as I learned from my parents, to give a child the feeling from the very beginning that it's his duty to take over. The heir to a family business is not a free agent. I'm the family trustee. I have a fiduciary function. My inheritance is not mine.'

The family has no motto, or none the count remembers. He quotes a saying of Goethe's instead: 'Was du ererbt von deinen Vätern, erwirb es, um es zu besitzen – what you have inherited from your forefathers, acquire it, in order to possess it. I understand the meaning of that now.'

THE LADY VANISHES
Veruschka, Body Painter

The rambling house stands well back from the road at the end of a village in Bavaria, about an hour's drive from Munich. You can't miss it, Veruschka promised on the telephone. And you can't. It's painted a spectacular shade of red, a warm and inviting colour, as if it had been soaked in claret.

Drowsy, bucolic, the doorbell must eventually have produced a sound somewhere inside the house. After a minute or two, when this no longer seems certain, a window opens above and an elderly lady peers out. She'll be down right away, says the lady with a smile; and the tall, supple figure in faded black slacks and blouse who is already emerging from the claret-mellowed house, creating a spasm of colour, is unmistakably Veruschka.

Vera Lehndorff, alias Veruschka, the fashion model who had an internationally successful career during the 1960s and 1970s, has led a secluded life here for much of the past ten years. The house used to be inhabited by monks, she explains as we enter a bare corridor with whitewashed walls and a vaulted thirteenth-century ceiling, and begin to climb uncarpeted flights of stairs. Monkish austerity is still in evidence. The austerity continues right to the top of the house, but with the profane sculptures we encounter on the way gradually ceases to be monkish. Her mother (that was her at the window) lives on the first floor. On the floor above, a resident artist has an apartment at one end of the landing; a famous actress, non-resident but sometimes in need of privacy, has a hideaway at the other.

ENCOUNTERS

There's an apartment for guests. And Veruschka's own den, in a converted attic.

A sign on the door announces in French 'When a woman says no, she means no'. On the far side of the door, apparently undeterred by any possibility of being vetoed, another artist is waiting to meet us. He is Holger Trülzsch, an old friend of Veruschka's, and her artistic collaborator: the two of them have made a name for themselves for the paintings they do on Veruschka's body.

How does one get started on body-painting? In the engagingly bohemian atmosphere of her attic, surrounded by a fertile chaos of photographs, paintings, bricks and stones arranged in purposeful ruins, she sketches the fluctuations of her extremely eventful life.

Born into the aristocracy of East Prussia (now Russia), where her ancestors had been landowners for six hundred years, the infant Vera was fortunate to survive the war. Separated from her mother and sisters after her father was executed for his part in Stauffenberg's attempted assassination of Hitler, she was not reunited with her family until the war was over. They were now refugees. They had lost everything.

In desolate post-war Germany the fatherless family began the nomadic wanderings that continued throughout her childhood. She went to thirteen different schools.

'We lived like gypsies,' she says. 'Naturally it was not a very happy time.' And after a pause she adds with characteristic energy, 'But I have got all that behind me now.'

She has been interested in painting nearly all her life. It was as an eighteen-year-old in Florence, where she had gone to teach herelf to paint, that she got her first job as a model. 'Somebody just happened to ask me to do some pictures. Then I began to get involved in modelling, because I thought: maybe not a bad idea to make some money! I thought of using the possibilities of transformation that a model has as a kind of stage. Perhaps I was something of an actress manquée. If I'd gone into acting

I might have expressed, in acting, those interests that now have a different outlet.'

What soon distinguished Veruschka the model was not just her striking appearance and athletic figure. It was the attitude she brought to her work, a desire to participate actively in the whole process of creating images, from the location and the props to technicalities of lenses and the quality of light. In partnership with star photographers such as Richard Avedon and David Bailey she sought to break away from commercial modelling and to make pictures that were original and interesting in their own right.

She is emphatic about her need to be independent. 'I didn't want my image to be controlled by the commercial interests who'd bought me. Really, they kind of *buy* you. I resisted being commercialised.'

At this juncture the photographer who has been hovering in the background, keeping an anxious eye on the clouds building up outside the window, declares his own commercial interest in taking a few pictures before the light fades irrecoverably. She agrees with a laugh (the technical argument is impeccable), and we all troop back downstairs.

It's already started to rain. Conveniently, there is a canopy out in the garden with a dais and two rudimentary throne-like chairs, in readiness either for sunshine or for a performance of Greek tragedy, but the photographer ignores what is merely convenient. Claret-coloured wall in the background is irresistible. So Holger and Veruschka sit out in the rain, a few yards from the canopy, and have their pictures taken wet. Soon the rain is pelting down. The photographer calls for an umbrella. It is brought out and held over the camera.

'Cat! Wonderful! We must have the cat!' exclaims the photographer. Startled, everyone looks round. Sure enough, a cat has ventured out into the rain and is watching our antics without much enthusiasm. Veruschka says the cat won't have its picture taken just to please us, but to oblige the photographer she tries to coax it on to her lap. The cat promptly unfurls its tail and stalks off disdainfully. 'See? I told you so!' Veruschka seems to approve of the cat's independence.

The photo session continues upstairs in the attic. In defiance of the unseasonable weather, Veruschka hands round sunshine glasses of champagne sherbet, ice cold, as if we were sweltering in summer heat. While she and the photographer are setting up the picture, Holger resumes the story.

He first met Vera in 1970. He came to the house with a friend, with whom he had an electronic music and percussion group, to make a recording for an LP. He had studied at art college in Munich, but was equally interested in music, and a project he had already completed, 'Sound sculptures in open and closed space', sought to combine both interests.

'I had my sound sculptures in a farmhouse in Tyrol. They were beginning to be a bit of a problem, because even the vibrations of someone walking across a room could trigger them off. Bing! Bing! Or that whispering effect you get in electronic music. It was weird. I had to wrap napkins round the sounding parts if I wanted to be undisturbed.'

When he and Vera met she had already experimented with body-painting. At first it was just as an accessory to modelling. She began changing the appearance of her skin, painting it different colours, in search of new transformations, new images. But the first real body-painting she did was for an Italian film in 1968, entitled, appropriately enough, *Veruschka*. The image shows her head, painted like a stone, surrounded by other stones, of which it seems to have become a stony part.

'It was my idea to do it. At that time it was simply a way to – ' she pauses, gropes for words, 'to escape just being always a human being. I felt trapped somehow. Being photographed all the time, I wanted to hide. I didn't want to be me. I don't know what it means to be just one person. I've always worked with different images of myself . . .'

Holger contributed other ideas, other images and painting

skills, adapting the techniques of fresco, of astonishing virtuosity. Holger, of course, takes the photographs of the finished product, but the actual painting of Veruschka's body is a joint undertaking in which they are both equally involved.

An example of their earlier work is a series of pictures called Mimicry, which forms the opening section of their book *Veruschka, Trans-figurations* (Thames & Hudson). It is a clever, brilliantly executed series of images that show a variety of costumes (and hence persona) painted on to Veruschka's naked body, teasing our notions of reality and illusion.

In one sequence she parodies a striptease, successfully deceiving the eye and at the same time making a mockery of its deception: paint has merely been added and then taken away from a body that remains naked throughout. The images of Veruschka posing as a man are cynical and disturbing. In the portraits of raffish, elegantly decadent young men, touting cigars and pistols and even gloating over the centrefold of a porn magazine, we always remain aware of the naked female body on to which these chimera have been projected.

These transformations are a logical continuation of the work Veruschka had been doing as a model, but with her metamorphosis into exotic birds and creatures, and in particular with her semi-incarnations as inanimate objects in a corroding industrial environment (in their book this sequence is called Oxydation), she and Holger have broken new ground.

It must be laborious, physically strenuous work. She may have to pose for as long as sixteen hours, her body covered with layers of paint, generating an awful lot of heat. Is there much satisfaction in that? No, says Veruschka with her spontaneous laugh, that part of it is actually rather boring. She needs the photographic image. It is only afterwards, when she can see what she has become, that the complex feelings urging her to make these pictures are given a kind of satisfaction.

We look at examples from the Oxydation series: Veruschka

painted cracked-blue and rust-brown, merging with a cracked-blue and rust-brown iron girder behind her; Veruschka mottled, blotched, chequered, striped, fusing with a variety of mottled and blotched backgrounds. Sometimes the superimposition is complete, with pipes appearing to sprout from her knees, a strip of flex running down her shoulder to a light-switch on her breast: they look as if they were actually there, she seems to have become the extension of these things. In the next picture we see her moved a little to one side, revealing the switch, flex or door-handle painted on her to be three-dimensional objects behind her. The effect of these slight shifts in perspective is powerful and uncanny.

When she looks at these trans-figurations, as she calls them, does she have more strongly the feeling of herself disappearing, or of having become something else?

'Oh, become. It's like going into matter. I sometimes thought I was coming through that wall. I feel I have done a journey through things. As a child, I used to feel an unbridgeable distance between myself and other things. I remember embracing a tree, hoping to become a tree myself. As an adult, of course, I know it would sound ridiculous to say I wanted to become these things.'

Wary of psychological interpretations of their work, Holger describes what he gets out of it with intellectual detachment. 'Working with Vera allows me to paint in a traditional way, to paint exactly what I see, on her body. Until I met her I did not know how to get back to figurative painting. But in this way I can escape the conflict of the modern artist, who finds himself forced into the abstract and away from the figurative, the joy of being connected with the object.'

After fifteen years of body-painting, what direction will the Lehndorff-Trülzsch partnership take in future? In their recent work the symbiosis of Veruschka's body and the background into which it has been painted seems to have reached the point where she will soon disappear into it altogether. A photo hanging on her attic wall purports to show Veruschka embedded in mountains of cloth in a warehouse in Prato, where second-hand clothes are sorted for recycling, but it's impossible to make her out. Is her final transfiguration an allegory? A picture of the clothes without the emperor?

With her finger Veruschka traces the outline of an invisible woman concealed in the piles of rags. 'See? The final transfiguration will be the picture where we'll say I'm there but I no longer am.'

NEW CLOTHES FOR OLD
The Rag Trade in Prato

It is almost as if the mountain of rags I have been keeping an eye on for the past half hour were alive; a self-depleting organism, steadily taking itself apart.

Pieces of cloth fly off left, right and centre, landing in half a dozen subsidiary heaps that grow as the mountain shrinks. The centrifugal force at the centre of the mountain gradually comes into view, in the shape of a small, dusty demon of a man with hollow cheeks and burning eyes, wearing a woollen cap and windcheater that look very much as if they have been appropriated from one of the previous heaps the man has sorted. As the pile diminishes, so does he. He crouches, soon he is folded up and sitting back on his heels, soon, amazingly, that mountain has been sorted in its entirety, according to quality and colour, down to the bare warehouse floor. A minute later a fork-lift truck deposits in front of the man another mountain. He gets to his feet and starts all over again.

What happens to those cast-off clothes that disappear on the back of the rag-dealer's truck? If they have any wool in them it's as likely as not they will arrive in Prato, a city of one hundred and sixty thousand inhabitants just outside Florence, which has been processing wool for the past eight hundred years, and a world centre for reclaiming wool since the turn of the nineteenth century. A share of them will arrive for sorting at the premises of Roberto Morganti on the outskirts of town.

Morganti is a familiar type of Prato businessman – a dealer in stracci, the Italian term for rags, second-hand clothes and industrial textile waste. Less familiar these days is Morganti's confidence, as evidenced by his modern warehouse with an area of over five thousand square metres built only two years ago, in the future of a declining trade that many expect will eventually die out altogether in Prato.

The long, complex process of reclaiming wool, from sorting, carbonising, grinding and dyeing the rags from which recycled yarn is spun to the weaving and fulling of the finished cloth, might be taken as a paradigm of that never-ending cycle of change underlying the existence of all things; and the stracci warehouse where this process begins, or the cycle is resumed, might equally supply a contemporary illustration of the myth of Sisyphus.

Sixty to seventy tons of rags pass in and out of Morganti's warehouse every day. They come from all over the world. After carbonising, a process combining heat and hydrochloric acid to eliminate vegetable and cellulose impurities such as cotton, linen, rayon and so on, the wool reclaimed from the rags is spun and woven in much the usual way.

Fork-lift trucks pile the incoming bales in walls of rag as much as ten yards high. They whizz up and down a labyrinth of narrow passages, taking away here, adding there, fetching and carrying like busy insects, shifting a brilliant kaleidoscope of textiles, multi-coloured mountains intersected by deep-red ravines, corridors of pure green, an astonishing topography of cloths and colours that is never quite the same from one minute to the next, and of which every single item will pass through the sorters' hands.

It is the relics of people's lives the sorters handle – eiderdowns, jackets, coats, pullovers and cardigans, so identifiably, poignantly human in the piles on the warehouse floor. Labels sometimes betray their provenance; a child's pullover of one hundred percent Shetland wool, a cashmere cardigan from a shop in Burlington Arcade, a piece of sacking from the Ivory Coast. But the sorters don't need labels. They take a second or two to scan the composition of fibres with their fingertips. Some of them, like Morganti's star performer Sergio, can tell the percentages of woollen and synthetic fibres at a glance.

Sergio – even the name, echoing serge, of the dusty man with the burning eyes binds him to the trade he has followed for thirty years since he began at the age of fifteen. He is eyes and fingertips in a trance of cloth, the rest of him out of focus. Fifteen is the age at which to learn the craft; at twenty still just possible, at twenty-five already too late. Sergio's colour sense is phenomenal, says Morganti, his voice breaking with emotion, an infallibility that comes not from experience but passion. Passion? Si, the sensuous scrutiny of cloth is a passion.

A fork-lift truck showers another load of rags at our feet. Sergio sorts between one and a half and two tons a day. In his working lifetime so far well over ten thousand tons must have passed through his hands. His answers to questions are terse, stoic. Yes, his father was in the trade before him. No, he would like his own children to study. The cold in the warehouse, the hours of kneeling, the strain on the eyes – you get used to it, he says. And then there's the unexpected bonus one always finds in old clothes. Hardly a week passes in which the sorters don't pool sums of a hundred to a hundred and fifty pounds they find in pockets or sewn into linings. People don't like to pay taxes, explains Sergio. I ask him if he also has a nice collection of cashmeres at home. Sergio glances quizzically at his boss, perhaps working out his percentages, but Morganti smiles and waves his arm with an expansive gesture that encompasses the millions of rags in his warehouse.

Andrea Balestri, a one-man thinktank behind the nameplate of a research organisation called Pratofutura, is less sanguine than Morganti about the future of stracci or of the Prato textile industry in general. Paid to ask uncomfortable questions, he is coming up with some uncomfortable answers.

A quarter of a million people live in the Prato textile area. About half of its working population, accounting for around twenty percent of the turnover value of Italy's annual textile production, depends on the industry for a living. Almost two-thirds of the area's textile production consists of yarns and cloths for apparel, of which two-thirds again are woollen material for winter wear. Thus Prato's industrial structure not only lacks diversification in general, but is heavily biased to wool processing within the textile industry in particular. Nowadays the problem for the world's largest woollen spinning area is ironically located at the source of its wealth and former pride – too great a dependence on wool.

At around three hundred and fifty grams per yard, wool is a relatively heavy fabric. Many of the clothes we wear today, Balestri says, are made up of vegetable and synthetic fibres with a weight per yard of around two hundred grams. People living in heated houses and moving about in heated cars naturally prefer lighter fabrics, a preference that is increasingly being taken up by textile fashions. Wool is also a more traditional material, associated with conservative design and colour, putting it at a disadvantage in a fashion market dictated by the ever growing requirements of informal wear. The problems of weight, weakness and slow drying inherent in the properties of wool can be overcome with worsted yarns, but Prato's is an exclusively woollen yarn industry. Fifteen years ago sixty percent of its raw material consisted of wool reclaimed from stracci, today it is twenty percent. Because of the decline of the market there is no incentive to invest in new woollen spinning machines, encumbering the industry's future still further with gradually obsolescent technology.

Since the early 1980s employment in the textile district of Prato, which stretches over the territories of ten 'municipalities' of Tuscany, has been on the decline. In the course of the 1990s, Pratofutura predicts, some fifteen thousand of the area's fifty-five thousand textile employees, or almost one third, will have become redundant.

No ripples of this dire prediction can be detected as yet

on the surface of the city's placid, prosperous life. In front of the Palazzo Comunale stands the statue of Francesco di Marco Datini, the fourteenth-century merchant and founder of Prato's affluence, since whose time the saying goes that if you look under the foundations of the city walls you will find a tuft of wool. Walking from here along the streets surrounding the Piazza del Duomo at the city centre, I find such a surfeit of textile stores that I wonder where the residents buy something to eat.

But people in the trade are unmistakably worried. Of the fourteen thousand textile establishments in the area, ten thousand are individual, artisan-type businesses concerned with just one specialist function of textile processing and employing only a handful of workers. Danilo Ceabatti, close to retirement age and with no heirs to follow him, sees the writing on the wall of his half-deserted carbonising plant, magnificently decaying since the turn of the century. Others, like the Rafamelli family, who operate in their back yard a warping machine that winds from five thousand spindles a fantastic tangle of yarns on to the warp beam for the loom, or the Nenciarini brothers from a family of weavers with eight looms running at ninety decibels in a thunderous shed, owners of small businesses such as these complain of a sharp downturn in trade during the last couple of years and don't know whether they are in the trough of just another of those cycles endemic in the textile industry, or whether their existence is fundamentally at stake.

'Natural selection – the fittest will survive,' says Piero Bellucci, not at all disconcerted by last year's twenty-five percent drop in the turnover of the cloth-making business he inherited from his father. Fashionably disdaining cuff-links, he sits at a desk in front of what must be an extremely expensive picture by Sandro Chia. Bellucci's company is one of the Big Five, each generating more than fifty billion lire in Prato's annual textile turnover of four thousand billion.

The remarkable feature of Prato's industrial infrastructure is the smallness and specialisation of its component units. Even Bellucci, employing one hundred and seventy people directly and seven hundred as sub-contractors, is not a big company by the standards of the textile industry worldwide. Competition is here less of an issue than co-existence, the inter-dependence of a complex industrial symbiosis in which Bellucci needs the Nenciarini brothers and their loom shed almost as much as they need him.

Bellucci thinks that the former strength of Prato's industry is now its weakness – the production of middle and low grade fabrics in huge quantities, quantities allegedly of an order that would suffice to unravel bolts of cloth continuously to the moon and back several times over. That business has now been lost to more competitive manufacturers in southeast Asia, and yet half of Prato's cloths for apparel is still graded for the mass consumer market.

Bellucci sees the answer to their problems in concentrating on fashion, quality and design. A third of the textiles his company produces already goes into spring and summer collections, employing silk, linen, cotton and synthetic yarns, and no wool at all. Fashion-oriented makers of cloth must be flexible and react fast – a staggering eighty thousand new textile designs are generated in Prato every six months. Quality fashion means shorter production runs, cloths in quantities not of tens of thousands or even thousands of yards but as little as a hundred. Computerised warping machines and looms could facilitate the costly, time-consuming adjustments required ever more frequently by short production runs. Maybe in the Nenciarini brothers' shed?

'E' giusto! We need the small artisan outfits, because they can be much more flexible to fluctuating demand than the bigger companies. Prato has gone wrong because the banks have been investing in the wrong places. It's not necessarily the smaller firms that will die out. It's the firms that continue to produce low-grade cloths in large quantities and fail to respond to the challenges of the new market.'

ENCOUNTERS

This is the moment in our conversation when I feel I must broach the word stracci, which in Prato these days, I have come to realise, is acquiring the sort of undesirable flavour imparted to adversaries' names so memorably by Mafia bosses in *Some Like it Hot*. What place is there for scrap clothes in this higher order of textile things that companies like Bellucci now envisage? Is an apotheosis imaginable, whereby rags recycled from Morganti's warehouse are eventually elevated to Armani's bosom?

Energetically Bellucci distances himself from this heresy, but otherwise his view of stracci is refreshingly pragmatic. Leaving the question of their unsavoury image on one side, he explains that the problem with stracci is largely an economic one – quantity and quality of supply are insufficient, processing is too labour-intensive, the yield of reclaimed wool is too low because of the increased blend with synthetic fibres, and costs are accordingly too high. Sensibly, therefore, the Pratese cloth merchants now get rid of half of the stracci they used to spin and weave in its entirety by the expedient of exporting it abroad.

With excellent growth rates expected in 1988, Bellucci faces the future coolly, at least where his own company is concerned. What is still not clear to me, and maybe not to Bellucci either, is the fate of those fifteen thousand textile employees predicted to be out of work fairly soon. So I pay a last visit to Andrea Balestri to sound out Pratofutura's forecasts; and also, I hope, to reclaim my coat, which I think I have left in his office.

The coat isn't there. Forecasts, or scenarios, as Balestri more tentatively calls them, are available in four designs, but all of them still seem to me to beg the question of alternative employment. Prato's future may lie in a technology-intensive textile industry specialising in computerised design; in an artisan-style industry with the emphasis on handcrafted quality cloth; in shifting production to developing countries, the local industry concentrating exclusively on design and skilled finishing; or in a gradual decline of the textile industry altogether, to be offset by moves into related fields such as the manufacture of textile machinery. Whatever way, it looks as if the flexibility for which Prato is famous will be a quality much in demand.

My coat can only be at the stracci warehouse. In the meantime it may have been processed through the shredding machine and is now on its way to be carbonised. But there's a chance, depending on just where I left it, that I shall be able to reclaim it before Morganti does. And I'm twice lucky. Prudently Sergio has laid it on one side, with a tiny volume entitled *La cosa piu' grande del mondo*, which he has fished out of his rags this morning as a souvenir. What, the booklet enquires on page one, is the Supreme Good to be sought in life? Cashmere, I'm tempted to say under the circumstances, but on page two the author sides with Corinthians and declares it to be Charity. A verdict with which Roberto Morganti and his colleagues in the rag trade would probably agree.

A MAGIC TOUCH
The World Magic Congress in Madrid

For the customs' officials at Madrid airport it must have been a mystifying week. Does any tourist nowadays need three top hats? Why this sudden plethora of rabbits, cats, cockatoos and doves in the hand luggage of so many travellers? What is the taxable value of this costly casket, unfortunately perforated with holes, or of a silver-topped cane which dissolves before one's eyes into a silk scarf? Is it a scarf, señor, or a cane? It is neither of these. Resisting taxable scrutiny, it vanishes altogether in a puff of smoke.

Twelve hundred magicians from over thirty countries have descended on the Spanish capital in early July for the World Magic Congress, held every three years under the auspices of the International Federation of Magic Societies. In the course of six days and nights seventy invited artists will demonstrate their skills in seven gala shows, a further one hundred and forty manipulators, mentalists, close-up magicians, magicians general and grand illusionists will be competing for the Federation's prestigious awards. There will be lectures on such handy topics as cutting and restoring a rope without scissors or glue, on the fine art of levitating blondes or the coarser craft of sawing them in half. Downstairs, at the Magic Fair, members of the fraternity have a choice of forty stands to pick up the newest tricks of the trade. We are all set for a magic marathon.

Or most of us are. There have been a few casualties. In the foyer of the Congress Palace Bob Brown from Sacramento, California, approaches with despondent face. Reality, in the form of Spanish customs and excise, has interposed itself between Bob and his illusion: his props have been impounded.

'They want a deposit of three thousand dollars. Heck! And we're on tomorrow.'

He's on with his partner Brenda, an uncanny blonde who has not visibly aged since the congress in Brussels six years ago. Bob has levitated Brenda in many of the capital cities of the world, but Madrid will enjoy the distinction of seeing her impaled on a sword. This is a new and interesting twist to their professional relationship.

Scantily clad, as always in public, Brenda awaits her fate coolly in front of the office of the organising committee. She has other worries on her mind. 'And don't forget the rabbit. Okay? We need a rabbit . . .'

There are a lot of delegates who need something from the organising committee, and frequently it is something which the committee appears unable to supply – organisation. Lack of organisation is available, in generous quantities, with a splendid Spanish blend of dignity and weariness which impartial observers learn to accept and even to admire.

But the Swedish manipulator whose clenched fist is now resting on the counter is neither impartial nor an observer. He is a competitor. Or he thought he was. He should have gone on yesterday, but his props went astray in Amsterdam. Having recovered his props this morning, he now learns that he may have forfeited his right to compete. His face chills.

'But I *must* compete. I have practised my act for three years!'

'There is no must,' admonishes the committee gently, placing his registration form on a shelf out of harm's reach. 'We will see what we can do.'

A sympathetic colleague advises the Swedish manipulator to explore other channels. Perhaps the general secretary can intervene on his behalf. Or someone on the honorary committee. They scan the programme for important sounding titles and helpful looking faces until they settle on the portrait of a man with an eminently responsible face and a warmly reassuring smile. Yes, this is their man.

It is the face of the honorary president of the congress, Felipe Gonzalez Marquez, better known outside magic circles as the president of the government of Spain.

There is time for a drink at the bar. It is quarter to four, and the afternoon competitions are not scheduled to begin until three. Spanish punctuality is reliable. Everything begins one hour late.

Ron Macmillan, a dealer from London with an illustrious magic past, is peering with an expression of mild surprise into his empty glass. I wonder if he is inducing it to replenish itself. Instead I ask why so few British magicians have entered for the competitions. Is there a dearth of talent? Ron wiggles his head intriguingly. He won't commit himself on that. But it costs a packet, doesn't it, to get yourself out to Madrid and stay there for a week. Beyond most aspiring magicians' means. But the dealers have found it worth their while to come over from England. Quite a few of them at the Fair.

And how did he get all his stuff through customs? The old manipulator's hand weaves sinuously through the air. He grins. 'Magic.'

A glassy middle-distance stare, suggestive of hypnosis, simultaneously transfixes the faces of all the waiters behind the bar. The closed-circuit televisions have been switched on, the afternoon programme has begun. Magic is in the air, there is no escaping it, not even in the bar.

On stage an enormous speckled egg is in the process of hatching itelf. The sharply serrated shell opens, like jaws, to reveal a hairy orange creature with shining globular eyes. The act that issues from the egg is not always easy to follow, the magic not always identifiable, but for bizarre originality I feel it deserves a prize.

Appropriately enough, the egg motif is developed in sub-
sequent acts by magicians specialising in Bird Productions; a
Japanese competitor with ducks, a competitor from Columbia
with doves. No problem in getting the birds to appear. The
problem is in retrieving them. The ducks are enjoying the
unexpected freedom of the stage. They resist incarceration.
The doves take a graceful turn through the twilight of the
auditorium.

Max Oscar from Austria, in the category of General Magic,
evidently has a drinking problem. He is already swaying when
he comes on stage, and he will be a lot drunker when he
leaves it. He plucks a glass from the air, tosses it off, another
leaps remorselessly into his hand. Six drinks materialise in as
many minutes, and he drains them all. It is an illusion of
alcoholism which does not lack reality. In the intermission
that follows I do not go to the bar. I take a peek backstage.

The orange creature is sitting cross-legged on a bench,
leisurely swinging webbed feet. It consists of two persons,
although the programme advertises it as one. They have removed
their eyeballs, worn on stage as helmets, and hold them quaintly
in their laps. The left eyeball introduces himself as Brujulo. In
real life his name is Ramon and he works as a TV actor. The
right eyeball wears spectacles. He is Ortega, the unadvertised
part. He has also entered for the Mental Magic competition
under the name of Don Alberto, 'to confuse the jury', he
explains. Ortega alias Don Alberto says that his real name is
Jesus and that he makes a living selling air-conditioning, but
his training is in electronics. He pauses for me to digest this.
Magic is a bit of a wheeze, he adds.

In the corridor outside the stage door the diminutive Japanese
magician is packing and labelling his magic coffers. He has
travelled the thousands of miles from Nagoya to Madrid for
a ten-minute performance that has ended in a fiasco.

'Because of the ducks. Ga ga ga ga ga ga ga! Very unruly,

Spanish duck! You see?' And I do. Fluttering his hands and swooping forward, he does an impressive imitation of a Spanish duck.

It transpires that the Japanese magician and the Spanish ducks became acquainted only this morning at a farm on the outskirts of Madrid where he leased them for his act. What can one expect from leased ducks with undisciplined farmyard instincts? He bears them no ill-will. And he is utterly undismayed.

'To perform on a stage like that . . . it was the greatest moment of my life.'

His eyes shine. It is not heroism. He is telling the truth.

For most of the competitors, with no hope of a prize, performing at the congress is like placing their flag on the Everest of the magic world. To perform in front of an entirely professional audience requires courage, a resilient brand of exhibitionism and in some cases, it seems, an element of masochism.

The audience knows how the trick is done. It has come to see how well it is done. It is kindly disposed, but it reserves its applause for pace, style and very special dexterity. It is indefatigable, always in the hope of seeing something new, something different, perhaps even – the ultimate illusion, the magician's grail – something inexplicable.

Day after day the fraternity watches dozens of Zombie Floating Balls rise unaided and fall; Multiplying Billiard Balls materialise between fingers; solid rings link and unlink; ropes knotted, cut and restored; cigarettes, cards, dogs, candles, cats, cockatoos and doves produced in dizzy profusion from silks, hats, newspapers and gloves, from a flash and a puff of smoke. The variations are endless, the repertoire arcane.

There is something eerie about this congress: illusions presented on behalf of illusionists who are undeceived by the appearances.

Magicians are entertainers. Some of them are amateurs primarily entertaining themselves. Some are professionals entertaining others. In a lay audience, at least, the reaction they elicit is always the same: astonishment. This is a very satisfying reaction. It is instant recognition. For a lot of magicians, apparently, a need for recognition becomes addictive. Perhaps this helps to explain why the delegates to a magic congress display a more single-minded dedication to the purpose for which they have been brought together than at any other kind of professional gathering I have attended.

No time out, over a drink at the end of the day, to scan the newspaper headlines or exchange experiences of post-Franco Spain. I am at once distracted from any such pursuits by a man with lugubrious, reptilian eyes who festoons my trousers with safety-pins before we have even spoken a word. Introductions are unnecessary here. The trick identifies the man.

He is Pablo Segobriga, doyen of Spanish close-up magicians. Close-up magic is magic done literally under one's nose. It is being done now. Pablo links and unlinks solid, clasped safety-pins six inches from my eyes. With a touch he looses them from their fixed anchorage on my trousers and threads a glittering silver chain. Then he sticks out his tongue at me. He is not being rude. It is in order to burn his tongue, slowly, caressingly, in the flame of his lighter.

How long has Pablo been doing such things? Fifty years. The sad face loses itelf briefly in a mocking smile; the hands grope for the support of a cane. It is not a magician's cane.

And later, at the reception given by the mayor of Madrid in the Cecilio Rodriguez gardens, where, intriguingly, 'gentlemen are requested to present themselves in costume', the announcement that the mayor cannot appear in person but has arranged for a substitute is applauded by the assembled illusionists with unequivocal professional sympathy.

The stars are out, the lanterns lit, the tables spread. A magical evening.

The Japanese magician, hapless with ducks, has no eyes for any of this. He is watching the peacocks parading brilliantly down the avenues with an interest that I feel may be very ill-advised.

'The Standard Wrist Chopper comes at £25.'

Mid-morning at the Magic Fair, where Martin Macmillan, son of Ron, is kindly showing me round the stand.

'Would you like a demonstration? Bill, could you . . .'

People go to extraordinary lengths to sell their wares. Bill sacrifices his hand.

'Or how about the Magic Bar? Very handy for parties and only £35. Endless supply of drinks, you see . . . those? The broomsticks? That's the Broomstick Suspension. A nice levitation at £295.'

Sawing a woman in half costs a bit more. All original and custom made. Martin fondles his instruments of torture with a craftsman's pride. The model his hand is resting on is the Slimline Saw'em Thru. And that cabinet in the corner is the Mismade Girl, for truncation and reassembly in four parts, 'depending on how you want to do it. For Comedy you do it different.' Very nicely finished, I say. Magicians like a good finish, says Martin.

On my way through the foyer, in search of a lady magician for a quote on the feminist point of view, I see that the Swedish manipulator is still, or again, at grips with the organising committee. Even at a distance of fifty yards the committee's extravagant Latin gestures make plain that it is washing its hands of the matter.

Back stage, however, there have been more encouraging developments. Brenda is rehearsing being impaled on a sword. So Bob has succeeded in bailing out their equipment.

What is the feminist point of view on – ?

'Hi. Just wait till I get off this sword.'

I wander out into the corridor, where a woman with a cigarette in her mouth and an aerial resting against her shoulder is stationed outside the stage door. But she is busy too. With frantic speed she is flicking alternate switches on what appears to be a radio transmitter. How curious. I sidle into the auditorium, but the Mental Magic number has unfortunately just come to a close.

A professional magic audience does not sit idly and watch. It engages in active scrutiny. No fiddling around with puny opera glasses here. I notice various members of the audience focusing their attention on the stage with the aid of powerful binoculars. This is not merely an advantage. Sometimes it is indispensable. Certain magic acts remind one of Hans Andersen's tale of the emperor's suit of clothes. A French manipulator is going through the motions of making things appear and disappear, or I assume he is, for I never actually see anything at all.

A mid-afternoon glaze settles over the auditorium, but by six o'clock we are all perky and back in our seats for the five o'clock gala show. Here is our host, the deft and jolly Marc Metral, to present the invited artists and take us through his own ventriloquist's routine. Thus, ingeniously, it is through the mouth of a dog, not a dummy, but a live talking animal, that the muttered exasperation of the congress is ventilated at last and the organising committee given a public carpeting – to the huge delight of the audience.

The magic adrenalin is flowing now. We are in just the mood to appreciate the sensational Impaled Beyond Belief. We are spooked by Jeff McBryde's magic parable of a man who gets trapped in his own illusions. And the laughter at the sight of Otto Wesseley coshing a dummy rabbit and tossing it disdainfully into a dustbin explodes as heartfelt deliverance. The magic congress is parodying itself.

Refreshed after their half-day excursion to Aranjuez, where they have been treated to the incruent bullfighting of a capea and to a candle-lit dinner in the arena afterwards, the magicians arrive bright and early on the final day of the congress. Even the Swedish manipulator is looking relaxed. The committee has finally relented and agreed to give him another chance. Perhaps the president of Spain has interceded on his behalf.

The tail-enders of the competition are put through their hoops at a cracking pace. The slothful genius of Spanish administration rallies, appears to vindicate itself at last.

Then we wait several hours for the announcement of the prizes.

To the accompaniment of slow clapping, three men clamber on to the stage. Their leader speaks with magnificent solemnity. He praises the jury. He praises the organising committee. He praises everyone he can think of. Imponderables, he discloses finally, have been the cause of this most unfortunate delay. He passes the microphone to his colleagues, who instantly relay this masterly verdict in English and French.

The prizegiving ceremony is one of the better Comedy Magic acts we have seen. The master of ceremonies gets his notes mixed up, makes wrong statements, forgets names. The audience is inured to embarrassment, but it is extremely piqued, for the first time at this congress, to learn that almost half the prizes will remain mere illusions. No first prize for Manipulation, no first or second prize for the Grand Illusion and no prize at all in the category of Invention. This declaration of the bankruptcy of magic is only made available in English and French. Mobbed by the audience for a Spanish translation, the MC snaps back testily that French and Spanish are so nearly the same that further translation is surely superflous. The auditorium is instantly in uproar.

At this point the festive evening cracks and begins to disintegrate.

Imponderables, again, delay the start of the prizewinners' gala by three hours. Davido's doves, when they eventually appear, are unable to bring peace to the audience. Angelico's comedy act can hardly summon sufficient energy to raise a laugh. The

most engaging part of the Turrini family's Grand Illusion is
their resemblance to the Three Musketeers in pyjamas. In
the long, and gradually longer, intervals between each act the
presenter of the show, an Egyptian sorcerer reputed to speak
sixteen languages, blunders up and down the proscenium in
various guises of increasing absurdity in an attempt to rouse
the audience from its apathy. His credit with the audience is
already low, as a result of his having forgotten, apparently in
sixteen languages, the names of the prizewinners it is his job
to announce; and soon he has forfeited it altogether.

Two male spectators are summoned on stage to serve as
illustrations of the sorcerer's unusual magic tastes. He causes
objects to disappear and reappear in various places about their
persons. When this place turns out to be one of the gentleman's
private parts, and the sorcerer brazenly commences to open his
trousers, the audience leaps to its feet in outrage, part of it quits
the auditorium altogether, the sorcerer is hissed from the stage,
missiles are hurled from the galleries and for a long time the
theatre is plunged into total darkness.

'And now ladies and gentlemen – please, please – presenting
the new world champion . . .'

The voice echoes out to a corner of the foyer where for
the past six days a cigarette vendor with mournful eyes has
been sitting patiently beside his wares. The vendor's corner
has acquired an addition, a mysterious cardboard box which
was not there this morning. We open the flaps of the box. A
white rabbit is sitting inside. Somehow its ears seem familiar.
Isn't this . . .? Surely she can't have forgotten – ?

But Brenda is already teetering over on high heels.

'The rabbit! It's got to have a carrot, something to drink.
The poor darling!'

She takes the vendor by the arm, indicates the rabbit and
conveys, in pantomime, her wish that it be given something
to eat and drink. The vendor nods his head enthusiastically.
There is the risk of a tragic misunderstanding here.

ENCOUNTERS

'Oh, no! How horrible! He might be thinking I'm saying he can *eat* the rabbit? How the heck d'you say lettuce in Spanish?'

Fortunately the cigarette vendor speaks French, and the misunderstanding is averted. Brenda is happy. The man is happy. He will take the rabbit home as a pet, and that will make his daughter happy. The gala show is over, the magicians stream through the foyer and disappear into the Spanish night. They look happy too.

The rabbit is probably happiest of all. It has awoken from a nightmare. It will never want to see the inside of a top hat again.

POKER FEZ

Amarillo Slim and Co. at the All Moroccan Championship

I t's only a hundred miles to the Sahara, and looking down from the top of La Mamounia Hotel at the red city of the medina with its huddle of sun-blasted buildings and ramparts made of beaten clay, one could imagine that the desert had once migrated north, got rained on and dried out thereafter as Marrakesh. In summer the thermometer here can be pushing a hundred and fifty degrees. Spring is the season to travel. Temperatures are coasting in the low eighties, bougainvillea and oleander are in their freshest bloom, the unchanging city haze of ochre and desert-pink is briefly startled by a splash of white – the tents erected in the vicinity of the palace gardens to accommodate those loyal subjects who have travelled from all over Morocco for the anniversary of the coronation of their king.

Coincidentally, as Arab princes are checking in at the La Mamounia and desert tribesmen are parking their camels in the souks, jets are landing at Marrakesh airport to unload the loyal troopers of another travelling show. They have travelled thousands of miles from California, Nevada and New York, from Dublin, London and the Midlands. Some of them set out unsure what continent they were headed for and checked it on a map in flight. The only king here they are going to get at all excited about will be the king looking up from a playing card. These troopers are in town to compete for the first ever Moroccan Championship at the Golden Oasis Poker Tournament.

The hosting of a poker tournament in a Moslem country,

where gambling is forbidden under Islamic law, is itself a gambler's proposition of no mean order. No Moroccans, unless Christian or Jew, will even be able to participate in what an outfit from Birmingham called Gaming Tournament Promotions Ltd. has gallingly advertised as their national championship. 'Odds are a foreigner'll win it,' observes a punter laconically, 'probably an American, possibly by the name of Johnny Chan or Amarillo Slim.'

Johnny Chan may be the reigning world champion, but to most of the estimated seventy million Americans who play poker the name Amarillo 'Slim' Preston is still probably worth a few chips more. The difference is between being famous and being a legend. These days, with the long arm of the Ayatollah Khomeini hovering over the green baize and Gadafy rumoured to be in and out of town, any Americans, let alone gamblers, intrepid enough to have penetrated Moslem territory might be advised to keep a low profile, but low profiles are not Slim's strongest suit.

The cowboy at the entrance to the Grand Casino La Mamounia stands six feet four, the Stetson he is invariably wearing must top him off at around seven. Slim? Even words like lean or rangy hang loosely on him. He's been memorably called the advance man for a famine, a description that emerges even more memorably through his Texan drawl as 'Heck, when ah was a kid ah had to git out the bath tub 'fore ah pulled the plug.'

After Nick the Greek and Titanic Thompson, Slim belongs to a brontosaurian species of gambler, hustler and scallywag extraordinaire that regrettably seems to be on its way out. 'Get a lot of it,' was Preston Senior's advice to young Slim, and the sixty-five odd years of his life have been spent doing exactly that.

After early years touring the world as a pool-playing child prodigy, Slim's career was profitably interrupted by a spell as a black marketeer in post-war Europe, got back on the road in the southern states, where he and his cronies moved in on the towns 'like vacuum cleaners' for whatever they could take at pool, dominoes, craps or poker tables, until he achieved, with prosperity, a flush of respectability as the owner of a clutch of ranches and a chain of fast food stores. It takes a man of bluff to call a bluff, and Slim's sayings such as 'Play the player, not the hand', or 'What ah could smell cookin' warn't on the fire' can usefully be borne in mind when on the receiving end of yarns about how he played pool against Minnesota Fats and licked him with a broomstick or took the owner of Hustler magazine, Larry Flint, for nearly two million dollars at a poker game where the chips were stacked 'higher than a dawg could jump over'.

Characteristically, Slim is in town with his travelling companion Larry Saunders, who runs the card room at Caesar's Palace in Las Vegas, to raise the American profile by a yard or two. Within hours of their arrival archaic water carriers can be observed lolling under palm trees, still looking a little incredulous in Caesar's Palace baseball caps and shiny black polyester jackets. And there's a lot more cooking on the old scallywag's fire.

'Few years back,' says Larry with a grin, as he watches Slim sizing up the casino entrance, 'Slim brought his horses up from Texas for a cutting horse event at Lake Tahoe. And you know what? Rode one of those darned horses right into the casino, for a fact he did. Well, we're in Africa, right? So what I figured . . .'

Larry's bet is on for a thousand bucks.

The surrounding Moroccan desert teems with mirages. For a week Las Vegas becomes one of them. With its Persian carpets the size of tennis courts, Art Deco furnishings, Andalusian patios in the style of Alhambra and allegedly no prospect of recouping the seventy million dollars outlay recently spent on refurbishing for about the next hundred years, La Mamounia Hotel itself is not doing too badly in the mirage stakes. While Slim melts into the background in search of tractable camels, champion

ENCOUNTERS

Johnny Chan is pacing Carrara marble mausoleums disguised as hotel corridors in pursuit of the ultimate Las Vegan wraith – the sucker riding in from the desert with billfolds the size of bricks and an amateur's sporting interest in a game or two of poker. On Day One he's still shaping up nicely, is leaving, has left, will be here any minute, the mysterious Monsieur G, multi-millionaire from Paris. On Day Two he's melting fast. Garbled rumours that read like the ingredients of some lunatic quiz, involving the Eiffel Tower, a falling window sash and a severed fingertip, quickly disperse to reveal the sensational non-appearance of Monsieur G. Exit Johnny Chan.

Faces from London, Birmingham, Wolverhampton etc. brighten up around the poker table. The Moroccan Championship is up for grabs, the trophy already enshrined on the mantelpiece. Jauntily the Brits don flower-pot hats and call this variant of the game poker fez – not without a certain piquancy. Among the surprising number of self-styled businessmen here whose professional activities can be defined as elastically as Moroccan timetables no one is actually travelling incognito, but no one came just for the publicity either.

An enterprising exception is Anthony Holden Ltd., on holiday from real life for a year in order to write a book about being a professional poker player. Take a careful look at Tony, already profiled by the *Las Vegas Review-Journal* and billed by the brochure for the forthcoming World Series as one of poker's rising stars, and you'll see a man with diamond-studded eyes: a sure sign of mirage fever. Short odds are being quoted that the book may take longer than a year, even that its author will disappear inside it altogether.

Poker is a singularity in the universe, a black hole with an infinite capacity for absorbing time, money and any residual sense of place. At the witching hour of dusk, when the guide books advise Marrakesh tourists to admire the harmony of the koutoubia minaret and ponder the secret of those magical numbers on which its medieval architecture was based, the poker tourists are calculating the odds on drawing to a flush on fifth street or pondering magical numbers which at best will add up to a low straight. From dusk to dawn, for twelve of twenty-four hours seven days in succession, the hypnotic dance of cards continues back and forth across the green baize, a choreography subtly changing with the names of games that to an outsider mean nothing – Short Deck Stud, Draw, Omaha, Seven Card Stud and Hold 'Em poker.

Slim clinches the first tournament game, mysteriously fades thereafter. He's off his form, the cards aren't running for him, whatever. A pungent smell of camel he brings with him to the table suggests his mind may be on other things. A bull-necked London bookie without a name is showing strong on the outside lane and places second on two successive nights. Still biding his time at the back of the field is another bookie, this time from Dublin and with a string of credits to his very presentable Irish name – Donnacha O'dea, former Olympic swimmer, maybe one of the best three players in Europe, definitely one of the most affable troopers orbiting the international poker circuit. Jack and John, two plenty tough looking loners from Nevada, pick up the scent of the poker trail in Casablanca, materialise overnight among a spray of dollars like the greening of a desert, dematerialise at dawn with empty pockets. A minister from Kuwait, a prince to boot, appears in the casino to a resounding riffle of expectant chips, turns magnificently on his heel and disappears with his dirhams still intact. Two more mirage makers, Californian real estate developers Howard 'Tahoe' Andrews and David Belluci, are still transatlantic. Meanwhile, back on the ranch, enter Eric Drache on a white charger, unseating the opposition on three consecutive nights.

'Where am I? How did I do last night?'

It could be the morning-after question of any itinerant gambling man. When Eric asks it he seems to be looking for an answer to his life. He graduated to poker from tossing marbles and spinning baseball cards while he was still a kid – too young, he thinks, not to start playing poker but to be able to understand the game as depending on finely calculated odds. He untwists the apparently inseparable double helix of pokergamble and impales the distinction on the prongs of a syllogism: 'Gambling is wagering unfavourable odds. Poker is wagering favourable odds. Therefore poker isn't gambling.'

In three tournament games, each lasting five to six hours, Eric picks up around thirty thousand dollars or a quarter of the total prize money. This doesn't answer his question, however, because at the side-games accumulating around midnight his money will again submerge in pots for as much as three times that amount, and even these sums have to be seen in the perspective of the world-class professional Eric undoubtedly is. For Eric the night is not yet over. It never was. It never will be.

The six hundred dollars he originally invested in a Las Vegas weekend had been converted into seventy thousand dollars within a couple of months. At the crap tables he began wagering unfavourable odds, recouped at poker, won and lost, won and lost for twenty years. 'I guess the ratio now is forty-five:forty-six – you guess which is which.' Tracking the ellipses of the money involved is a job not for an accountant but an astronomer.

Either way, it somehow doesn't seem to matter. It would be hard to find a more democratic constitution than the one that applies to the United Republic of Poker, and Eric Drache, unsalaried organiser of the World Series, has emerged as its ambassador to the world because he embodies its spirit best – an even-handed insouciance, by no means carelessness, born of a gut philosophy that life is a precarious form of liquidity anyway, in the long run can neither be won nor lost, and is accordingly most enjoyable by just keeping the chips in circulation.

The ten players who sit down to contest the All Moroccan Championship and prize money of nearly thirty-four thousand dollars to be divided on a sliding scale among the first three are all very much in favour of keeping their money in circulation – for days, if necessary for weeks. The tournament game, however, is freeze-out Hold 'Em, which in about six hours will guarantee at least the illusion of losers and winners. The players receive two cards face down, combining them with five communal cards rolled three-one-one face up in the middle, folding, checking or raising in the intervals between deals. Each player buys himself into the game – or herself, if she were there – with a two and a half thousand dollar stake. Every hour the antes are raised, and for the first two hours players who have lost their initial stake can buy themselves another two and a half thousand dollars worth of ammunition as many times as they care to risk. Thereafter it's sudden death, at best a temporary reprieve.

In accordance with the most fastidious poker standards in the world, i.e. Las Vegas etiquette, all the players are dressed to kill, which in seven and a half cases out of ten means sweatshirts, sneakers and reasonably grimy pants. The professional smiles of the casino staff became redundant a week ago and have smudged as a permanent wince. Unorthodox in his ambassadorial status is Eric Drache, astonishingly sporting a jacket and tie. The Legend is a law unto himself. Slim wears a pink shirt with uncut emerald buttons, two further emeralds glitter in the eyes of the rattlesnake that bit him a decade ago and has remained coiled around the dome of his Stetson ever since. Its jaws are open, the fangs waiting to strike, but it leaves Slim to do the talking.

'Hey you Britishers out there, tell me s'more about that word "mate". Where ah come from we jes use it for breedin' animals.'

Ninety percent of this sniping banter, by turns hilarious, lunatic and utterly outrageous, is also quite unprintable. On those unused to it the effect can be devastating. Slim in spate is a one-man stampede. The first to go under is a man from Birmingham, soon followed by the bull-necked bookie, who picks himself up bloodied and bristling with rage. David Bellucci has prudently corked the ear on the Slim side of his head with an ear-phone, a drip-feed containing a taped Inner Voice to wipe that fork-tongued cowboy out, but this doesn't help either. He, too, crushed, despite a sound level of wealth against which the dropping of thirty or forty thousand dollars at a single game is barely audible. It's not the money that matters. It's the pride of fiercely competitive men who've been given a whipping. Tahoe, too, disentangles himself from the game looking like a man who met a bear in the middle of a briar patch. 'How do I feel? Like I'd bought a property that just got hit by an earthquake.'

'Sheee-it! Believe me, boy – I *ain't* got no heart!'

'I believe you, Slim. You don't have a heart in your whole body.'

Slim has met his match. Slim has just met a talking Irishman with a charming smile and a pair of aces.

Get thee behind me, Slim. Tony Holden does, beating him to fifth place, rising gracefully when his two queens get mugged by three villainous knaves from the West Midlands; while Eric, who has been nodding off at intervals throughout the game, finally falls asleep in fourth place. An Irish bookie, an English businessman, and a Sikh by the name of Cinders . . . the joke would take an hour to tell. Forget it. The sensational and wholly absurd punchline is that the trophy of the first Moroccan Poker Championship now rests on a mantelpiece at an undisclosed address in darkest Hertfordshire.

In the Legendary Scallywag Stakes, however, Slim pulled off another coup. The camel baulked a bit at the slot machines, and given a couple of yards more neck would have nibbled at the leaves of a glittering tree disguised as a chandelier. Meanwhile the travelling poker circus moves on – to London, Louisiana, the Caribbean, the World Series in Las Vegas, the Isle of Man and maybe Cairo at the end of the year if by then it has got on to the map. Slim was last sighted in Rangoon, where he is reported to be negotiating the possibility of reviving defunct gambling establishments. He may not win the Burmese Poker Championship, but if there are any suckers around, odds are ol' Slim's gonna win himself a bet the size of an elephant.

GERMANY INCORPORATED
Student Duelling Fraternities

The students are on strike, the lecture on Einstein's special theory of relativity that the freshman Harald F would otherwise have attended has been cancelled as a result. He goes instead to the square at the city centre where thirty thousand people have gathered for the largest student demonstration ever held in the city. They are demonstrating for better facilities, more representation and cheaper accommodation at Munich's hopelessly overcrowded university.

Harald leaves the demo early and returns to his lodgings. Although he faces the same problems as any other student enrolled nowadays at one of West Germany's mass universities, accommodation is not one of them. Harald is a member of a Corps, an élite body among the various student Associations whose secret constitutions in some cases date back almost two hundred years. At the house owned by the Suevia Corps in Werneck Street, conveniently only a few minutes' walk from the university, he and a dozen other Corps probationers, or Füchse, as they are called, rent rooms at the extremely reasonable rate of twelve pounds a week.

Harald has other things on his mind. As a member of an Association he has not only privileges but duties, and as a member of a Fencing Association, which by their constitution all Corps are, one of those duties is to prove himself in a trial by sword – a ritual known as the Mensur. In order to be accepted as a full member of the Suevia Corps, Harald must voluntarily submit to this ritual not less than five times within the next couple of years. Today is his first time.

ENCOUNTERS

Eight combats have been scheduled for the evening. Harald secludes himself in his room and listens to music to help himself unwind. Or is it to wind up? 'A spot of Wagner will do the trick, I think.' He is on fifth. While the music of the *Walküre* leaks under Harald's door, the first combatant is already being dressed for battle in a room beside the kitchen.

The first article of protective gear is a high cloth collar, followed in successive layers by a jerkin made of a sort of sailcloth, a second chain-mail collar extending over the shoulders, a chain-mail shirt and a padded horse-hair apron, bloody with the gore of hundreds of previous sword bouts, to protect the lower half of the body. On top of this comes yet another collar, this time made of leather, a leather gauntlet from wrist to elbow, and a leather epaulette to prevent the sword-tip from getting entangled in the chain-mail shirt. Just before fencing the combatants also don metal goggles with a guard to protect the nose. In full fighting gear they bear a very authentic resemblance to medieval knights.

How does it feel inside? 'Damn hot.'

A Mensur is never fought against – strictly speaking, with – a member of one's own Corps. The opposite numbers invited for this evening's trial by sword are from the affiliated Corps Isaria. They arrive with their seconds and supporters; other members of other Corps whose bouts are also being hosted by Suevia this evening begin to traipse upstairs to the fencing room in the attic where the combats will take place. They all wear the striped caps and striped bands across the chest with the colours of their Association. They chat, joke and drink beer in a relaxed, clubbish atmosphere, not at all conspiratorial, reminiscent rather of a Junior Common Room.

Beside a table at the entrance to the attic room a doctor stands in readiness with steaming bowls of hot water, disinfectant, forceps, needle and thread and yards of bandage in case his services will be required. He is himself a Corps member, an Alter Herr, which can conveniently be translated as Old Boy.

Urbane, a little bored, he smokes a cheroot, entirely unaffected by the buzz of excitement around him as contestants and spectators throng in for the evening's first bout. He's been through all this before – hundreds of times.

So has Harald. At least, he has in training. The difference at a Mensur is that the fencer's head and face are unprotected by visor and helmet, and the combat sword is extremely sharp. Known as a Schläger, the weapon used exclusively by the student Fencing Associations has evolved from the épée – a sword about a yard long with a straight blade whose tip has been blunted.

Otherwise the Mensur procedure is exactly as in the previous months of training. It is laid down in a highly esoteric set of rules and regulations, known as the Comment, subtly differing from one Association to another, which has been fine-tuned in the course of many generations.

The combatants take up their positions a sword's length apart. They must be of the same height, and when this is not the case the shorter combatant stands on a platform to compensate the difference. One arm behind the back, feet planted apart, the fencers remain stationary throughout the entire bout. No movement is allowed apart from that of the sword arm. Even an involuntary flinching or drawing back of the head leads to disqualification, and the bout is declared invalid for the fencer who has 'dodged'.

By the book of the Munich Corps a bout consists of twenty rounds at the first Mensur, thirty rounds thereafter. In each round five strokes must be carried out. Fencing is done with the sword arm extended vertically above the head. Even in this artificially restricted position, allowing no more action than a flick of the wrist, there are seven basic and as many as thirty-five possible combinations of strokes, all aimed at the opponent's head.

And this is where blood will be drawn. Not at first. Patrick, Christopher and Harald, all of them freshmen probationers whose initiatory Mensur prohibits the use of more than the one elementary stroke, acquit themselves without 'dodging' or sustaining any injury. Smiling faces among the Suevians, some of them very relieved. They've got their lads through. Jokes, horse-play, champagne. Perhaps it is just a harmless ritual after all.

And for their last man it should also be a piece of cake. Fighting his second Mensur under Suevian colours, Joachim is in fact an old hand who has already fought four 'sharp' bouts under the colours of his former Corps at the university of Gießen. But Joachim's bout is over in thirty seconds – for just a careless fraction of a second he fails to close his guard sufficiently and the edge of his opponent's sword splits his forehead open in a gash three inches long requiring seven stitches.

The doctor has no time to light up another cheroot or drink a glass of champagne. Thereafter it comes thick and fast. In quick succession three stunned contestants emerge from the last three bouts with hands held up to stem the flow from bloodied heads. What looked as if it would be just a quiet evening of medieval fun and games ends very messily indeed.

In the official vocabulary of the Corps the word 'duel' does not and cannot exist. Privately, however, when passions are spent, the blood has been mopped up and all is said and done over a few pints of beer, opinions find expression that come very much into line with a point of view common sense would seem to indicate.

'No two ways about it,' says one of the students who has just fenced, 'the Mensur is a ritualised duel. Fatalities? The last occurred in the 1950s. By Mensur standards the wounds of the student who died were quite normal and harmless – or so it seemed. Only a freakish combination of secondary and tertiary causes, too long and complicated to relate, subsequently led to his death.'

The case also led to a verdict by the Federal Court, West Germany's highest jurisdictional instance, that the Mensur did not constitute a form of combat with lethal weapons, and was accordingly neither a legally punishable offence nor a socially unacceptable custom.

Intriguingly, then, the custom practised but never tolerated in any form since its origins in the middle ages first achieved official sanction in a post-war democratic constitution.

To describe the student Associations with all their arcane rituals as being typically German would be misleading. To call them simply a German phenomenon would be closer to the mark. The existence of Associations with broadly similar Mensur practices (or none at all) is nowadays confined to three west European, German-speaking countries: the Federal Republic itself, Austria and Switzerland. One author of a book on the subject of these 'academic corporations', the majority of which have neither the Mensur custom nor obligatory fencing, guesstimated their members in the early 1980s as numbering around a quarter of a million, almost two-thirds of them in Germany.

'The reasons are historical,' explains Bernd, the Old Boy in charge of the Corps archives. 'Students at medieval universities, where they travelled on long and dangerous journeys, were enrolled as members of "nationes". From the fourteenth century onwards, German-speaking scholars banded together for their mutual protection in groups known as Landsmannschaften – groups of fellow countrymen from that quiltwork of kingdoms and principalities which only very late, a few decades before the turn of the nineteenth century, were unified as a modern state. In the intervening centuries, and in response to divergent political currents surrounding that fundamental German issue of federalist coexistence versus united nationhood, the original Landsmannschaften of the universities were dissolved, reconstituted and gave rise to rival student bodies – the Corps and the so-called Burschenschaften.'

These are still the names today of the three Fencing Associations that in one form or another have retained the Mensur as the corner-stone of a still very traditional way of life. In common parlance members of these and other student Associations are loosely referred to as 'incorporated students'.

Why does a student want to be incorporated today – young men whose heads, when not entangled with swords, are likely to be busied with the theory of relativity or abstruse aspects of Common Market law?

Dinner punctually at seven o'clock with members of the Suevia Corps at their house in Werneck Street. Daily attendance is obligatory for probationers unless they have a very good excuse. The question goes round the table with the fish that a motherly housekeeper serves.

As an alternative to the loneliness, frustration and competition of life at a mass university, with over a hundred thousand students, in a city that in many cases is far from home. To find and keep acquaintances who'll remain intimate friends for the rest of one's life. To discover the true meaning of a comradeship it's impossible to experience any other way. Some of the answers are tinged with an idealism that sounds not merely plausible but convincing.

Others find more practical reasons. To learn something of the social graces, the sophistication or savoir vivre they think they may need in later life. To get to know girls. To become accustomed to public speaking. And connections on the Old Boy network, so helpful when looking for a job or advancing a career – do they perhaps also play a part? An Old Boy attending dinner weighs the somewhat awkward silence around him and says 'No doubt there's that aspect too. It may be an advantage. But in itself it's not a sufficient reason to want to join.'

Joining is sometimes a matter of chance. An acquaintance who is a Corps 'brother' may invite a student along. Often it's a case of family tradition: fathers and grandfathers were also incorporated. If the applicant finds acceptance among the other probationers he is accepted as a guest for several weeks. Only men need apply, of course. Thereafter, if the new probationer feels he belongs and the others feel so too, he becomes a Fuchs and wears the Corps colours – also in public, if he wishes, although experience shows that this is not advisable.

In Suevia's case a Fuchs will fight his first Mensur within a couple of months, his second towards the end of his first university year. He is then 'received' into the Corps as a Bursche, or fellow. After an examination lasting five or six hours he swears an oath on the secret constitution of the Corps. His status as a fellow is now symbolised by the three-coloured band the senior confers on him, which he will keep, cherish and wear on formal Corps occasions for the rest of his life. In the obituaries published in the Corps newspaper it is not the date of birth that is registered, but the date when the deceased was received into the Corps.

During his two to three years as a fully active member the Corps student must submit to the discipline of his highly organised community life. Apart from the rigours of the Mensur itself, fencing practice is compulsory five days a week. Every evening, after supper, one of the probationers will be picked out to give a summary of the most important topics of the day's newspaper. He must also acquire and memorise a vast body of esoteric knowledge concerning all details of the Corps' traditions. He will have to take restrictions of his personal freedom into account. Even in his own room, cheap as the rent is, he is not entirely his own master. Although a blind eye is occasionally turned, women visitors are not permitted. The time spent at meetings or on administrative matters is also considerable. And then there is the 'honour' question – the conduct considered fitting for a representative of a Corps.

Suevia, for example, has a checklist comprising such items as insufficient attention to one's studies, failure to comply with the request of a senior, unpaid debts in-house, drunken driving or contravention of a number of house rules whose breach a probationer is expected voluntarily to declare. In such cases the culprit is summoned to appear at the Corps weekly convention for disciplinary measures – usually suspension of the privilege to wear the Corps colours for a week or two.

'To most people that may not sound like a big deal,' comments Christoph, an Old Boy speaking from rueful experience, 'but within the closed community of the Corps it's tantamount to being branded as a felon.'

Even as an Old Boy, the former Corps student does not escape the reach of its vigilant councils. A man they considered to be guilty of breach of promise during an internal dispute that tarnished the Corps honour was dismissed as a result. The same fate was suffered recently by a Corps brother convicted of embezzlement. A particularly striking case was that of the Old Boy who chose to forfeit his membership in the Corps in the interests of his career under the Nazis. Forty years on he applied for readmission. The Corps refused – it has a long and unforgiving memory. Old Boys ostracised by fellow Corps brothers – cum infamia, in the most heinous instances – can thus effectively lose many of their life-long friends.

In the background there are always swords lurking. A form of the Mensur known as a pro-patria suit, formerly a duel fought when one Corps had been insulted by another and demanded 'satisfaction', nowadays little more, at least on the surface, than a sporting event taking place for merely formal reasons, can nonetheless still be invoked in the contemporary guise of the Mensur not merely as a formal ritual but in the authentic spirit of old-fashioned satisfaction. Individual members likewise have recourse to the Mensur, subject to the approval of their councils, when the honour of the Corps is at stake.

Christoph sums up: 'So although the Mensur doesn't qualify as a duel in the legal sense, it's still occasionally fought on grounds that are indistinguishable from the reasons that used to serve as pretexts for duels.'

Students who are members of Associations are gregarious, sociable people. If they weren't they wouldn't be where they are. Their life at university is a constant whirl of social events – conventions, banquets, booze-ups, the frequent rituals of their clubbish life to which outsiders are seldom or never admitted. But not only these. Cocktail evenings and skiing excursions, lectures, disco parties and dances that can go on all weekend are open to anyone members care to invite, their friends and most particularly their girlfriends. Shy probationers who have signed on as a way of getting better acquainted with the opposite sex soon find they've turned up trumps. A head count of lovely women who show up in revealing evening gowns for the annual Ball of the Corps probably scores much higher than can be expected at the average social occasion.

'Girls are intrigued,' says one Old Boy, 'much quicker than men to ask if they can come along to watch the fencing practice. Some of them don't approve of us, but I've yet to meet a woman who wasn't at least curious.'

Macho stuff. Disapproval would be a mild word to summarise the attitude of today's feminists. Surprisingly few people in Germany actually have any idea of what goes on inside the student Associations, but a poll of don't-knows seems to suggest that women's attitudes may be rather more tolerant than men's. Men sufficiently interested in the Corps to take a closer look at their activities will either want to join them or give them a wide berth afterwards, whereas girls who enjoy pretty clothes and parties and feel at ease in a conservative atmosphere can both have their cake and eat it. Quite possibly it will turn out to be a wedding cake.

Corps students are eligible young bachelors, typically with solid, bankable careers ahead of them in medicine, business or law. There is the odd technician or scientist among them, depending upon the particular Corps, even more oddly an artist or two, but these are not the most obvious marriage candidates. Just as many probationers are the sons of Old Boys, many of the young ladies glittering in the public orbit of Corps life are likewise Old Boys' daughters.

There is an element here of in-breeding, a perpetuity of

dynastic flow, from the cradle to the grave and beyond, in the continuity of filial succession. Neither social class nor money – the munificence of many an Old Boy reaches well beyond his annual subscription of a couple of hundred pounds – provides a stumbling-block nowadays to those who wish to be adopted by the family of the Corps. Poorer students are funded and pay no interest on their loans. No more is required than matriculation at the local university, good manners and loyalty to the cause. Once adopted, their services may be called on as godfathers at christenings, as best man at weddings where arching swords are held aloft for bride and groom to pass through, as pall-bearers at funerals, this time with swords lowered to the grave in valedictory salute.

To some people's surprise, and quite a lot of people's distaste, the student Associations and many of their traditions were disinterred from the rubble of defeat at the end of the last war. Until the mid-1960s their representatives dominated on the student administration councils at the universities, but in the years of student agitation thereafter they lost not only their political mandate, they lost touch altogether. The intake of new probationers dwindled. Some corporations closed down altogether.

With the change from a socialist to a conservative government in the early 1980s, and with the wind of a broader social change that then began to blow over the heads of a new generation of students who cut their hair and cleaned their clothes, the Associations limped up out of the trough and began climbing. The very private nature of these organisations makes it risky to venture any generalisations, but on the evidence of the nineteen Munich Corps, far more than in any other city, they're now in better shape than they have been for a long time.

Scum. Beer slobs. Right-wing intriguers. Highly suspect. Downright silly. Nationalist manipulators. Complacent sods. Reactionary bunch. Very rum blokes. Violent mob of militants. Chauvinists. Careerists. A relic of the past.

A sample of views on the street in front of Munich University is overwhelmingly negative. The few students with anything to say in defence of their incorporated colleagues belong to a tiny minority of outsiders with first-hand experience. The Corps may feel themselves in good shape. Their reputation is not.

'Our Mensur practices are widely misunderstood' – the complaint is as applicable now as it was a hundred years ago, when it was made by Kaiser Wilhelm II, an incorporated student as were his two earlier contemporaries, Bismarck and Karl Marx. Examples of incorporated students of such utterly different political persuasions as Bismarck and Marx can also be found nowadays. Hanns Martin Schleyer, chairman of the powerful Association of Employers who was murdered in 1977, was incorporated as was the terrorist Horst Mahler, then behind bars and awaiting trial as a member of the group of assassins responsible for Schleyer's death.

Between Corps, Burschenschaft, Landsmannschaft and the many Catholic Associations there are political differences that are commonly overlooked; differences between a liberal and a reactionary conservatism.

The Burschenschaften, for example, expect their members to subscribe to a similar political creed with an unmistakable nationalist bias. Foreigners will not be accepted as members, nor will conscientious objectors who refuse to do national service. Their political ideals encompass the reunification of Germany, which effectively excludes from their organisation any liberal, let alone any socialist point of view.

'In the Corps, by contrast,' argues Christoph, very sensitive to the distinctions outsiders fail to register, 'there exists a sort of gentleman's agreement that a member's politics are his own business. If we insist on any political principle, it's the principle of political tolerance. There's nothing on our statutes preventing a communist, a foreigner or a conscientious objector from becoming a member. At recent Land elections in Bavaria

the Suevia Corps fielded candidates from three political parties –
including the Greens, who are known as conservationists strictly
in the ecological sense.'

Whether justifiably or not, the negative opinion of the Associations held by the German public results from two running
sores: the ooze of nationalist sentiment and the whiff of élitist
privilege. To younger men and women of the post-war generation,
glancing over their shoulders at all the horrors perpetrated in the
name of National Socialism, the existence of a group of people
who cut each other about the face with swords, swear on secret
constitutions in dark places and beerily sing songs about the love
of freedom, friendship, fatherland and nation, even if those songs
originated centuries ago about a nation that then did not even
exist, serves as a reminder of a since discredited patriotism that
arouses feelings of deep unease.

The whiff of élitist privilege is less strong nowadays than it
used to be in Bismarck's time. It's said that something like two
thirds of the Prussian administration around the turn of the
century were recruited from the ranks of incorporated students.
But the sense of constituting an élite is still part of the ethos,
perhaps more so in the Corps than in the other Associations.
And although a statistically negligible quantity in the present-day
population, their representation in positions of power is still
disproportionately high.

Chancellors and their ministers in the post-war government
of Austria have in many cases been Old Boys of student Associations. In Germany the line of leading post-war politicians
who were incorporated students runs from the Republic's first
chancellor, Konrad Adenauer, to at least one prominent member
of the Social Democratic party currently in opposition. Leading
industrialists like the chairman of BMW, leading politicians such
as the recently ousted mayor of Berlin and members of the Senate,
the prime minister of Hessen and members of his cabinet, past
and present ministers in the government of Bavaria, the recent
president of the Bundestag, judges sitting in the Federal Court,

cardinals and even – as an honorary member – a pope, have all been incorporated in one or another of the Associations.

Protectionism? An irrefusable offer discreetly made via the Old Boy network? There's a case, but the charge would be hard to prove. But in a society not exactly noted for casual, easy-going standards, what other young people about to embark on a career have the benefit of such a huge circle of acquaintances in influential positions in all walks of life with whom they can be on intimate terms from the very start?

Fifty, sixty years on, the Old Boys still come back. In the candle-lit cellars of Suevia's house over a hundred men assemble to celebrate the anniversary of the founding of the Corps. All wear coloured caps and bands, the insignia of their Association. Probationers and still active seniors turn out in dark blue braided uniforms reminiscent of hussars'. 'Love and friendship first brought us together one hundred and eighty-five years ago today . . .'

Sketching in the sombre background of a hostile world outside, of which all those present are well aware, the Senior's commemorative speech reiterates loyalty to romantic ideals that originated during the Napoleonic wars, defends their continued relevance today. His audience registers its approval with a thunderous rumble of beer glasses on the bare wooden tables. More speeches and songs, from time to time the honoured company is called to order in Latin, swords and glasses are raised in florid toasts. The formal part of the evening ends with caps being impaled on swords, a ritual of swearing allegiance which is known as the Landesvater, named after the song that is sung in accompaniment.

Corps students have been impaling hats on swords as a symbol of allegiance for at least three hundred years. Nobody quite knows why. Like many of their traditions, its origins are obscure. Someone starts something, for no clear reason, and it just goes on and on. Maybe obscurity is a quality customs require in order to become traditions.

ENCOUNTERS

At the heart of the Corps life there is much that is inaccessible to rational analysis; nowhere more so than in the ritual of the Mensur. In the Corps philosophy it is justified as a test of fairness, courage, self-discipline, with neither winners nor losers. But behind this rationale there is something powerfully emotional, a matter just of feeling; something that can wake you up in the middle of the night in a cold sweat, galvanise your pulse to two hundred and twenty beats when you face the moment of truth. 'For me it can most honestly be described,' concludes an Old Boy, gazing dreamily into his glass, 'as the last real adventure of my life.'

The Sins of the Fathers
The Lost Generation of Niklas Frank

'The snapping of your neck spared me a screwed-up life, imagine the crap with which you would have poisoned my mind. Just as it has poisoned the silent majority of my generation, who were not fortunate enough to have their fathers hanged . . .'

Niklas Frank brings the coffee into the living-room and we sit down to breakfast in his country cottage an hour's drive from Hamburg, where he works as a reporter for the magazine *Stern*. Outside, a couple of sheep are grazing in the garden, the flat north German landscape rolls away and disappears in the mist.

'I'm very glad I grew up without my father.'

Somewhere on the far side of the mist, hundreds of miles to the east, lies Poland. Niklas Frank sees it in his memory. It is an occupied country, for the small boy who grew up there a giant toyland, courtesy of the Third Reich. His father, the governor general, resides like a king with his family in the fortress of Krakau. For six years the son lives like a prince in plundered splendour, indulgently watched over by SS guards. He plays hide-and-seek among the tombs of Poland's kings, drives pedal-cars down castle corridors and against the shins of staff who keep smiling on pain of death, lops off the heads of stinging-nettles with a diamond-studded sword. Perhaps there are also nettles along the patch of turf in Krakau where other sons of the Nazi invaders interrupt their football game when they hear voices singing the Polish national anthem beyond a row of houses, and shouting 'Hey! They're shooting some more Poles!' sprint to the corner as the machine guns briefly stutter, perhaps in time to see bloodied bodies still twitching by the wall where they faced the firing squad.

Niklas sits in the back of the Mercedes, holding nanny's hand. Mother is going on a shopping spree to the Krakau ghettos, those wartime supermarkets with wonderful discount prices specially for the Frank family. They make the most fancy little corsets, oh! they do, exclaims his mother rapturously, bargain-bound through narrow streets, lined with men in black uniforms and carrying whips. What pretty yellow stars the people wear on their arms. Why do they look so grim? But in pursuit of fancy corsets, furs, the knick-knacks of the ghetto boutiques, mother ignores the question. Niklas sticks his tongue out at the grim-faced people with yellow stars.

Much more fun is that afternoon in the place surrounded by barbed wire, where big fat men set frail and very thin men on a donkey and beat the donkey till it bucks, and the thin men fall off and are put back on the donkey and fall off again. Little Niklas laughs and laughs. They ceased to be funny long ago, but memories of that laughter will echo throughout his life.

He doesn't remember his father too well. The clearest memory is also the last. He visited him in the Nuremberg prison ten days before he was executed. His father lied to him that they would soon be spending a jolly Christmas all together, told silly stories and made jokes. The boy knew he was lying. He wanted the truth. He still wants it now. Forty years later he has written a book that must be one of the most savage indictments ever pronounced on a father by his son.

Why did he wait so long?

'I've always wanted to live to be older than my father. It has to do with the shame I felt, having my father hanged, you know, when I was a boy. My eldest brother felt the same. When he turned forty-seven he came to me and said: I'm older than Pa now. My sister said she wouldn't live to be older than father. And at forty-six she died of cancer. Maybe I have had to reach that age myself, in order to feel more free.'

The book takes the form of a remorseless interrogation of the father, whom the son envisages boiling in a cauldron in hell, racked by pains that might have been furnished by the imagination of a Hieronymus Bosch. It is a chronicle of the lies, brags, unscrupulous ambition, numbing heartlessness, petty and stupendous crimes, culminating in the rape of Poland and mass murder, for which Hans Frank, Poland's so-called Governor General during the war, was held co-responsible at the Nuremberg trials. It is difficult to find or even want to find anything to say in defence of this father. This son doesn't.

'There's hardly been a day in my life when I haven't thought about him, and always negatively, because always associated with those images that one carries around in one's head. Piles of corpses. Had I tried to write a straightforward biography it would have turned into a defence of my father, whether I wanted it or not, because even the most monstrous crimes can be explained. So I rummaged through my father's papers at random and let my imagination run, writing things down just as they came into my mind. Visions of him cooking in hell? Yes, I felt a pleasure in taking revenge. It was a good feeling to put the boot in. A child's disappointed love, maybe. The belated revolt of an adolescent, sticking his tongue out at God and feeling big. There's hardly a document or letter of his that doesn't drive me to fury. His cowardice, his loathsome servility, his reckless, altogether despicable character. Where was the man ever genuinely involved? Not even in his crimes. When judging my father it will always have to be by the heaps of corpses in Auschwitz. And compared with that any memories of cosy evenings when he was at home with his kids are worth absolutely nothing.'

Niklas Frank isn't looking for sympathy. He resists any suggestions that he might have had a rather difficult childhood. 'I

was never a victim.' His mother had to struggle to bring up the
five children in the hard years after the war. That she was
able to do so at all was largely thanks to the proceeds from
her husband's memoirs, written while he was in jail. The old
Nazis, now reinstated in democratic office, rallied round with
gifts, money, pious memories of the man they saw as a hero
who had been unjustly hanged.

A 'perfectly normal' childhood, then, followed in Bavaria,
tinged with fascist ideology in the home and a medieval Catholic
eschatology in the church, whose resources of imagery the author
Frank would later draw on fully. People in the village where
the family had to make do with modest quarters now that
their spacious country house had been confiscated no longer
tipped their caps and said 'Frau Minister' obsequiously when
his mother passed, but the Frank children went to the local
school and grew up on American Care parcels exactly as all
other German children did. Sometimes the name could be a
handicap. If a swastika had been chalked on the blackboard, it
was the Frank brothers who were at once assumed to be the
culprits and had to take the rap. The name also brought a
few perks. The cardinal sent his chauffeur in the eccleciastical
twelve-cylinder to pick the family up and bring them to the
archbishop's palace in Munich, where between banquet courses
absolution of good old father Frank was supplied gratis. This
kind of thing impressed the neighbours. And hitchhiking around
the country, Frank junior was also finding that people didn't
throw him out of the car when he told them who his dad was.
Quite the contrary. The magic password 'I am the son of . . .'
secured him a square meal, even some extra pocket money.

Nazi sympathisers also paid the boy's fees at a boarding-school
in north Germany, where he says he first encountered lingering,
or re-emergent, anti-Semitism; one of the very few charges,
incidentally, which he does not level at his parents. 'I grew up,'
he says, addressing his father, excoriated in the cauldron, 'in
an atmosphere of unmitigated appreciation of you and all your

works.' Among the older generation only his eldest brother was there to supply a better example, and he emigrated to Argentina the moment he left school.

For young Niklas the awakening came when adolescence ended and he enrolled as a student of law, which ironically had been his father's profession too. He sat in the law libraries, reading with feelings of disgust and shame the travesties of justice that his father, formerly Bavarian minister of justice and president of the academy of German law, had perpetrated by way of introductions to legal textbooks in the lawless 1930s.

This unpleasant experience coincided with a new requirement of adult life – filling in forms. Under Father's Profession he found it easier to write lawyer rather than former governor general of Poland, for Executed he naturally substituted Died. 'I didn't want the word to get around.' With fellow students he never discussed his father or the issues his father had represented. For nine years he immured himself at the university in silent anonymity, which was fortunately guaranteed by a very much more common name than Ribbentrop or Goebbels, dabbling in law, history, literature and the classical languages – emulating his father's broad humanistic learning, another legacy from which he cannot escape? – and left without a degree.

'I didn't know what I wanted to do. I didn't know what I wanted to become.'

One opportunity had already been lost while Niklas was still a student. His mother died, without Niklas having ever really sat down to talk to her about his father. Why?

'I sensed my mother had a bad conscience. And she wouldn't have been prepared to talk anyway. In recent years there have been a number of books by children of the post-war generation, people my age. This has to do with the fact that we feel guilty, guilty of having allowed our parents to get away with it. I didn't write a book just to lay bare my soul. I see it as a political book, motivated by the need to bring into the open the failure of our generation, the sons and daughters, to confront their parents with the past.'

Niklas Frank got married, found a job, started a family. For twenty years he suppressed the past. In the early 1980s, the years of the so-called political change in West Germany, when the conservatives ousted the socialists after more than a decade in power, he became curious to find out more about his father, and began to investigate the files he had so long neglected.

Contemporary events supplied the catalysis, events characterised by a political behaviour in which Frank identified 'an arrogance of power', reminding him of the ruthlessness of his father, whose career he was retracing at the time. He was alerted to what he saw as disquieting similarities in the use of politicians' language then and now, the methods employed to discredit political opponents, the demagogic appeals to crude instincts. The republic was rocked by a series of political scandals unprecedented in its brief history, culminating in the resignation and suicide of Uwe Barschel, prime minister of Schleswig-Holstein, whose career of lies, intrigue, corruption and perjury many West Germans still find it hard to believe.

Frank relates this bankruptcy of political morality to the conspiracy of silence that has buried the past. Touring the country in search of people who could tell him more about his father, he found himself being passed from one old Nazi to another, all of whom seemed to be very comfortably settled.

'For me there's a direct connection between our silence and such a disgraceful business as the Barschel affair – and Barschel belongs to my generation. We let our parents off the hook.'

This identification of cause and effect is plausible. Such ideas are common intellectual property in left-wing circles, but from his own rather special point of view Frank feels about them with unusual vehemence. 'Factually everything has been put on the record. What I miss are the emotions.'

The trouble is that his book about his father fails in its

ambition to point a contemporary political moral. His jaundiced view of the country he lives in – why didn't he emigrate like his brother? – is everywhere on display. Father and father country are alike submitted to the same unremittingly scathing review. Between the two there may be a connection, which Frank has overlooked. The political message, deserving the attention of a wider readership, is smothered under the intensely personal invective, a gross, fantastic outpouring, sometimes brutal and often so tasteless that readers are repelled who would have liked to come aboard.

He wrote the book for himself. A lot of people think he should have kept it to himself. 'My father was the roller of the typewriter on which I wrote it,' he says. The image is apt. He defends the grossness of his book as 'an act of violence' that was necessary to take his parents to task, not only the father whom he hardly knew, but also, and this was the far greater shock, the mother whom he thought he did. His portrayal of her in the book, based on the evidence of her own letters, shows a rapacious, hard-hearted woman, an accomplice in crime every bit his father's equal. At the age of nearly fifty, Niklas Frank has let the past in through a back door he had hitherto kept shut, detonating an explosion which has shaken the framework of his life.

'Disastrous,' is how he describes the reception his book has had in Germany. 'I didn't expect people to react so negatively.'

Whatever the outcome, at home or abroad, the fact that Frank has gone public with such a personal indictment of his parents is an act of considerable courage. At heart a private person, he finds the self-imposed publicity distasteful, quite apart from the fact that it is often of a hostile nature.

Although the book has not yet appeared in Poland, ironically because of paper shortage, Frank has been there to give interviews and make himself available to anyone who wished to talk to him. He was given a very friendly reception, he says. But in Poland it was probably inevitable that the shadows of the father's past would also reach out to embrace the son: in the form of the resistance fighters who had attempted to assassinate his father by blowing up his train carriage. They would do it again, they said, and would welcome the opportunity of blowing the son up with him. 'Quite understandably,' comments Frank quietly.

In Warsaw he stayed in a hotel near the tomb of the Unknown Soldier. He went there every day. Watching the passers-by pause there for a moment's contemplation, he discovered he felt envious of them. He envied the sense of national identity felt by a people who had fought a just war. And he quotes a remark he once heard made by an elderly German woman to a Jewish woman writer. 'You can mourn your dead. We are not allowed to do that.'

Since the appearance of his book he has travelled widely, giving public readings, which are often an ordeal for the reader and his audience alike. For the first time in his life he has had personal contact with Jews. At a reading in Vienna, hosted by the Jewish writer Peter Sichrovsky, there were many Jews in the audience. Elderly people, people who had come through the war. They sat there listening to Frank reading, the tears streaming down their faces.

Peter Sichrovsky contacted Frank to ask for his collaboration on his book project *Born Guilty*, a collection of interviews with the children and grandchildren of Nazi parents and grandparents, some of them small-time fascist opportunists, some of them internationally notorious war criminals.

Among the very different attitudes of the fourteen people he interviewed, Sichrovsky noted some experiences all interview partners had in common, and which apply equally to the case of Niklas Frank. In the homes of post-war Germany and Austria parents never discussed the past. They never expressed sentiments of personal guilt, shock or even shame. And the seeds of mistrust sown in the minds of their children by this conspiracy of silence have since burgeoned, if that is the word, into the suspicious pessimism that now characterises this generation's view of society.

How applicable does Frank find the title *Born Guilty*?

'I'm probably standing pretty much on my own when I say this but, yes, of course I feel guilty. I don't feel guilty for being the son of my particular father, which is merely a genetic coincidence, but I do feel guilty, as a member of the German people, for what the German people have done. Theodor Heuss put it very well: there may not be such a thing as collective guilt, but there is such a thing as collective shame. In 1933 we opted out of the community of nations. We're still not back in.'

We have finished breakfast. It's time to go. Outside it has begun to snow.

'I suppose I envy the people of all other nations, really,' says Frank wistfully. 'Sometimes I wish I'd been born the son of utterly different parents.'

THE GRAND ILLUSIONIST
On the Centenary of the Death of Ludwig II

T he commission encharged with taking the deposed king into custody arrived at Neuschwanstein Castle shortly before midnight. It was represented by the psychiatrist Dr Gudden, who only three days previously had signed the document testifying that His Royal Highness was mad, his assistant Dr Müller, a captain of the gendarmerie and five warders from a lunatic asylum. With the connivance of a valet they overpowered the king in the corridor leading to the tower room, where it was feared he might attempt to take his own life, and confined him to the royal chambers until preparations for the further journey had been made.

In half darkness, as day began to break, three coaches rolled out of the fore-court of Neuschwanstein down the forest road leading to Hohenschwangau in the valley. The royal passenger travelled alone in the second coach, from which the door handles on the inside had been removed, escorted by an outrider as a further precaution against attempts to escape. But the journey passed uneventfully. At noon the ominous cortege arrived at Schloß Berg, the king's residence on Lake Starnberg.

His Majesty was quartered in his suite on the second floor of the castle. He noted with distaste that peep-holes had been cut in the doors so that his keepers would be able to spy on him; and picking up a blunt golden fruit knife, as he sat down to dine, he inquired ironically if the usual order of the meal had been reversed and fruit was to be served at the beginning. When he had finished dining he retired to bed, with instructions to wake him nine hours later.

The doctors in attendance cancelled these instructions. The new regimen they had in mind for the royal patient would require him, like other mortals, to be awake during the day and to sleep during the night. Thus when he awoke towards midnight and demanded his clothes the warder on duty disregarded the order. The king walked up and down in his shirt, complaining peevishly of the cold, ate a piece of bread and an orange and retired to bed again.

In the course of the morning the king had further talks with Dr Gudden and Professor Grashey, another of the four signatories who had put their names to the declaration that His Majesty was insane. They outlined the measures they proposed to ensure their patient a speedy recovery, and he professed to be in agreement with their advice. His speech was clearly articulated, his manner friendly and even gracious, despite the fact that he considered the action taken against him to be an infamous plot and that he should have been consulted in advance. Why had the doctors neglected to examine him personally before pronouncing their verdict, basing it solely on the written statements of witnesses? Grashey replied that for many years past His Majesty had declined to see any doctors, let alone a psychiatrist, and had anyone attempted to subject him to such an examination he would probably have had him arrested. The king conceded with a smile that, indeed, such would no doubt have been the case.

After breakfast Gudden accompanied him on a walk through the lakeside park. A warder followed at a distance, with instructions to keep out of sight. Reporting the gist of their conversation to his colleagues afterwards, Gudden expressed satisfaction that the patient seemed to have come to terms with his situation remarkably well, and he sent an optimistic telegram to this effect to his political masters in Munich. Although fearful that an attempt might be made on his life, His Majesty was as docile as a child and would give them no trouble. Gudden's colleagues were less sanguine.

The king was served lunch in his chambers at half past four.

He ate with great appetite and drank beer, several glasses of wine and arrack. Having completed his dinner he sent for Gudden to accompany him on the second walk which they had planned for that afternoon.

At a quarter to seven the king and Gudden set off on their walk through the park along the lakeside path. It had been raining steadily for the past few days; both men wore a hat and carried an umbrella. Outside Schloß Berg Gudden intercepted the warder who had been assigned to follow them and ordered him to remain in the castle. He turned away hurriedly to catch up with the king. Soon the two men were out of sight.

An hour later, when they had still not returned, gendarmes were sent out to search the park, but on account of the driving rain and encroaching darkness it was not until ten o'clock that the first traces were found on the shore of the lake: the king's coat, jacket and umbrella and, further along the shore, two hats.

The search was continued by boat. Shortly after eleven o'clock the bodies of the king and Gudden were found floating face down on the surface of the lake in four to five feet of water, about twenty yards from the shore. The king's waterlogged watch, dangling from his waistcoat pocket, had stopped at six fifty-four. The two bodies were hauled into the boat and brought to the shore, where in the flickering light of the lanterns held up by the grooms and gendarmes who had assembled there attempts were made at artificial respiration. But rigor mortis had already set in before the corpses were retrieved from the lake. As the clock chimed midnight in nearby Starnberg, on 13 June 1886, the attendant doctor discontinued his attempts at respiration and formally pronounced the death of his colleague Dr Gudden and of His Majesty, King Ludwig II of Bavaria, in the forty-first year of his life.

Bruises on the neck and face of Dr Gudden, a torn fingernail, and footprints on the muddy floor of Lake Starnberg that were still visible the following day left the only record of the events of the previous night.

Apparently the king had broken through the thickets bordering the path and headed straight for the lake; Gudden had torn a fingernail in a vain attempt to stop him, for with one powerful leap forward the king had shed coat and jacket and taken huge strides out into the lake. Gudden pursued him. A fight must have taken place; the marks on Gudden's neck and face suggested that the king had forced his opponent under the water and throttled him. From this point a single set of footprints led out into the deeper water of the lake, where after a few yards they abruptly ceased.

Whether the king had stepped into the lake with the intention to escape or to take his own life can only be conjectured. It seems most unlikely that a giant of a man who was a strong swimmer could have succeeded so promptly in drowning himself in four or five feet of water. But although it was early summer, the water was still very cold – only twelve degrees. After the exertions of the previous minutes, the accumulated horrors of the preceding days, death had probably come to him, whether he had courted it or not, in the form of sudden heart failure.

How had this most majestic of kings come to such a furtive, ignominious end?

The verdict of contemporary psychiatry had pronounced Ludwig to be suffering from paranoia, which nowadays would be described as a form of schizophrenia. The report submitted by Gudden and his colleagues is marred by a number of deficiencies, not least of which was the failure to make allowances for the peculiarities of their patient's genealogy and the fact that he was a king.

With the exception of the Wittelsbacher princess Alexandra, who had been plagued by the painful illusion that she had swallowed a glass piano, the record of Ludwig's ancestors on the paternal side is relatively free of mental illness. But his mother, Princess Marie of Prussia, was the product of generations of inbreeding in the houses of Hohenzollern, Hannover and Brunswick. Examples of drastic emotional instability, fear, melancholy, misanthropy and weakness of character, litter the royal history of the generations preceding Marie and the son who became Ludwig II at the too youthful age of eighteen.

The withdrawn, serious, highly imaginative child was subjected by his father Maximilian to a spartan upbringing that isolated him from social companionship and thus exacerbated his natural proclivity to solitude. Pronounced differences of temperament estranged him at a very early age from almost all the members of his family. Towards his younger brother Otto he displayed those attitudes of regal grandeur that mushroomed during adult life into forms of megalomania which a nineteenth-century constitutional monarchy was no longer able to accommodate.

His childish companions were not people but objects, which he emblazoned with the proud heraldry of his imagination and warmed with his passionate blood. Foremost among these objects were the paintings and frescoes on the walls of the medieval ruin of Hohenschwangau which his father had bought in 1829 and restored as a family residence. 'A true fairy-tale castle,' remarked Ludwig's grandfather significantly, when he saw the building that had risen on the foundations of the ancient fortress.

In the murals of Hohenschwangau Ludwig encountered a fabulous procession of figures who stepped out of shadowy medieval legend into the living immediacy of his mind, embodying the ideals of loyalty, nobility and honour that inspired him throughout his life: Wieland and Biterolf, Dietrich von Bern and Charlemagne, and the Knight of the Swan, Lohengrin.

It was, therefore, extraordinarily fateful that the first opera Ludwig ever attended, at the age of fifteen, should have brought to the stage and thereby given a further reality to a world which had hitherto been confined to his own imagination. 'The Crown Prince was moved to tears of ecstasy,' a contemporary witness records, 'and in the solitude of his room or the park learned the text and all the composer's other dramas by heart.'

The composer was Richard Wagner, and the opera which had such a momentous effect on the prince was, of course, *Lohengrin*.

A few weeks after he came to the throne in 1864 Ludwig gave his councillor Pfistermeister a ruby ring and sent him out into the world to find one Richard Wagner. The envoy had instructions to hand the ring to Wagner with the courtly message that just as this ruby glowed, so too did King Ludwig glow with desire to meet the poet-composer of *Lohengrin*.

Wagner, meanwhile, was leading his creditors a not so merry chase back and forth across Europe. He had fled from Vienna to Munich, from Munich to Zürich and Mariafeld, and from there again to Stuttgart, where Pfistermeister eventually ran him to earth. But when an envoy of the King of Bavaria was announced, Wagner, disagreeably surprised that his secret arrival in Stuttgart was already known, took it to be some kind of prank and at first refused to see him.

And indeed, when the King of Bavaria, no less, clasped him to his bosom in the audience chamber of the Residenz in Munich on the following day, swearing an oath of eternal loyalty and promising him the riches of his kingdom, the penniless Wagner thought he must be dreaming.

Ludwig honoured his promise, continuing to support Wagner throughout the remaining nineteen years of his life. Under Ludwig's aegis, *Tristan*, *Meistersinger*, *Rheingold* and *Walküre* all received their first performance in Munich; and although the original plan to build the Wagner Festspielhaus in the Bavarian capital had to be abandoned, its eventual realisation in Bayreuth owed much to the donations of the privy purse. Without this royal patronage, Wagner later wrote, the Ring of the Nibelungen would never have been completed.

The relationship between two such outsize egotists could not have been other than stormy, and the storm began to brew at their very first meeting. Perhaps expecting the creator of

Lohengrin to be himself endowed with an almost godlike appearance, Ludwig was disappointed by the reality that at last confronted him in his palace: the reality of a small, ageing, ugly man.

The failure of mere mortality, even the mortality of a genius such as Wagner, to conform to the idealised expectations that Ludwig superimposed on his private relationships, vitiated not merely all his attempts at friendship but his ability to adjust to the realities of the world in general.

Nowhere is this underlying schizophrenia more evident than in the flow and ebb of his feelings for Wagner. In the rapturous outpourings of his letters he celebrated him as the Beloved One, my One-and-Everything, Saint, Redeemer, God; and yet, having precipitately summoned Wagner to his court, he avoided meeting him for weeks at a stretch. The differences between the two men are fundamental. Ludwig had a medieval understanding of kingship, Wagner was a republican with a revolutionary career behind him. For Wagner, the royal patron was a means to his artistic ends, while for Ludwig their relationship was a mystical bond, issuing from the fealty he had sworn not to Wagner but to the creator of *Lohengrin*.

The distinction was one that Wagner failed to appreciate, with fatal results. Confident of his influence over the youthful monarch, he meddled in politics and antagonised ministers already jealous of his intimacy with the king and scandalised by his high-handed behaviour. The citizens of Munich shared this antipathy, and the expulsion of Wagner from the court had soon become a political issue.

Ludwig could still have resisted this pressure and saved his favourite, had he chosen to. But he, too, despite the love he bore and would always bear Wagner, felt that his friend had overreached himself and trespassed, unforgivably, on the sacred prerogative of the sovereign. Thus he assented to the removal of the person who was closest to his lonely heart and soul after a sojourn at his court lasting only eighteen months.

*

'No words can describe the pain that rakes my heart,' wrote Ludwig to Wagner in the final letter before his friend's departure. It was the first disappointment in the young king's life and arguably it was the greatest.

From about this time he began to express that dislike of Munich which later became an almost pathological hatred. Throughout his life he avoided places with which he had unpleasant associations. During a summer he spent as a child in Berchtesgaden, for example, he had been reprimanded by a court official for treating his younger brother too roughly, and the humiliation of this reproach had so embittered him that despite his love of the wild beauty of the mountainous region of Upper Bavaria he never set foot in Berchtesgaden again. The slighting of Wagner by the people of Munich and ministerial encroachment on his royal privileges may have nurtured in Ludwig a similar distaste for his capital.

By his early twenties he had already established the nomadic lifestyle which drove his cabinet ministers to distraction. Court secretaries with urgent matters of state to communicate to His Majesty frequently had to travel to Schloß Berg or undertake the much longer coach journey to Hohenschwangau, documents of state requiring his signature were dispatched to hunting lodges in the Bavarian Alps and sometimes travelled perilously by water to the lake islands of the Roseninsel and Herrenchiemsee.

When war broke out between Prussia and Austria in 1866, a year after Wagner's departure, Ludwig was enjoying fireworks, jousting and amateur theatricals on his island in Lake Starnberg in the company of a groom and his adjutant Prince Thurn and Taxis. Bavaria was committed by treaty to enter the war on the Austrian side, and in order to discuss this urgent situation with the king the prime minister had to be ferried over to the island, where he encountered the monarch and his adjutant dressed up as Barbarossa and Lohengrin in a gloomy hall illuminated by artificial moonlight.

'Before our return to Munich,' Ludwig cabled to Wagner, 'which is occasioned by the events of the war, we feel the urge to send our warmest greetings from the Isle of Roses to our distant friends. How profoundly deplorable are the times we live in!'

Ludwig hated war and all things military in general, and he was distressed by war between the German principalities in particular. When Austria lost the war he smarted under the humiliation of the financial and territorial concessions which, as Austria's defeated ally, he was forced to make to Prussia. And even more odious than that: in the Prussian hegemony of German states for which Bismarck was striving he foresaw the shameful curbing of his kingdom and therewith of his personal authority.

Precisely the situation he had foreseen arose four years later in 1870. Bismarck astutely exploited the issue of succession to the Spanish throne as a means of manoeuvring France into a declaration of war. This time Bavaria fought on the victorious Prussian side, but Ludwig's bargaining position was not strengthened as a result. Bismarck's star was in the ascendant. Prussia emerged from the war as the indisputed leader of the confederation of German states, and with the investiture of Wilhelm I as Emperor in the hall of mirrors at Versailles the following year celebrated its apotheosis as the founder of a new German Reich.

'I'm in no mood to see a Prussian princess!' exclaimed Ludwig testily at the time diplomatic representations were being made to him to support his uncle's nomination as emperor. The princess whose request for an audience had provoked this impatient retort was his own mother.

And some years later, in his most lordly vein, 'She is merely my mother, and at the same time my subject.'

In the eyes of her imperious son, the Queen Mother embodied two antipathies which both became more violent as the years passed. She was a native of Prussia. And she was a woman.

The court and the common people followed the progress of the bachelor king's relationships with members of the opposite sex at first with sentimental interest, then with increasing concern, and finally resignation.

Ludwig was tall, dark and fabulously handsome. He had charisma. His mere appearance in public caused a sensation. Nineteenth-century ladies were restrained by decorum from mobbing their idols, but the wives and eligible daughters of Munich burghers were seen roaming through the corridors of the Residenz in the hope, if not actually of waylaying, at least of catching a glimpse of their king. Young ladies were known to be votaries of the portrait that adorned many a bedside shrine.

They, at least, must have felt a pang of regret when the twenty-one year-old monarch announced his engagement to his cousin Sophie Charlotte, Duchess of Bavaria. She was slim and graceful, with pretty features and rich golden hair, but these qualities probably interested Ludwig rather less than an enthusiasm which his fiancée shared: the operas of Richard Wagner. True to the self-dramatisation of his life in terms of Wagnerian drama, he had soon christened his young duchess Elsa and himself Heinrich.

Ludwig's insistence that his attachment to Sophie was a 'purely spiritual relationship' received scant sympathy from the girl's mother, who took it for granted that the flow of letters from the king to her daughter could be nothing other than declarations of love (as indeed they were, but for Richard Wagner). Only three days before the announcement of his engagement he had written her a letter in which he made it clear that he could not commit himself further as he had already dedicated his life to R. Wagner. Sophie's distress on receiving this letter softened Ludwig's heart. Circumstances beyond even his control forced his hand to a chivalrous gesture he had not really intended.

The engagement lasted ten months. Ludwig's public displays of affection for his declared bride failed to convince more perceptive observers. Franz Liszt, at a performance of *Tannhäuser* graced by the attendance of the young couple, noted darkly that 'les ardeurs matrimoniales de Sa Majesté semblent fort tempérées.' Ludwig was as indecisive about breaking the engagement as he had been in forming it. Only after repeated postponements of the wedding, humiliating for the bride, did he submit to the ultimatum presented by her father. A terse diary entry records his decision: 'Sophie written off.'

To Wagner he writes, 'I can breathe again, awake as from a dark dream, and now that the inner calm which was so long absent has returned once more to my soul I find myself close to my Friend again.'

Ludwig formed a much closer and more lasting attachment to Sophie's elder sister, Elisabeth, a childhood friend who became Empress of Austria. In the hundred years since Ludwig's death many legends have sprung up around this relationship, but in fact it was sustained by nothing more piquant than the happy compatibility of their natures. He paid court to her, in his chaste, swan-like, Lohengrin manner, and he probably enjoyed a greater intimacy with her than with any other woman. But he could afford to do so because it did not compromise him. The beautiful, vivacious Elisabeth, eight years his senior, had long been a married woman.

Ludwig's cloudy perception of women cannot be separated from the Wagner complex. It was the scheming of a woman, he implied sinisterly, which had succeeded in dislodging Wagner from his immediate life, and a dream he recorded in the year of his engagement elaborates this theme of a dark conspiracy of woman.

Herr von Bülow (the pianist and conductor whose wife Cosima eloped with Wagner) '. . . advised me to have *Lohengrin* performed in a hall to which no audience should be admitted, as on the previous day it had behaved very tactlessly; namely, hissing and shouting in such a manner that the overture could hardly be played to the end, and a lady had the impertinence to sing from one of the boxes insulting verses that made a public ridicule of me for having allowed such a work to be performed.'

As the dislike of women rose to the surface, the language of his dreams became correspondingly more explicit. The attendants at his truncated travelling court were later forbidden to appear in the company of their wives, in his dreams he maltreats the Queen Mother and hurls her down flights of stairs.

By the age of twenty-two Ludwig had already experienced the three brutal shocks which, opening his eyes to the realities of the world and of his own nature, dictated the strange course of his future life. He had failed to keep Wagner at his court. He had failed to defend the historic integrity of his kingdom against the maelstrom of Prussian imperialism. And he had failed in his relationship with women. What scope was there left his shrunken sovereignty, what was there left to do for a king who felt that there was no longer anything he wanted to rule?

He became a recluse, a shadow king. And he began to build castles.

In the winter garden of the Residenz the Grand Illusionist decreed the first of his pleasure-domes.

'A Himalayan landscape glowed out of the background, painted in such splendid perspective that even when one came right up to it the illusion remained undiminished. Huge palms of a breadth and beauty never seen in any hot-house, superb twining plants, the finest of the tropics, bordered an aisle that was doubled in the reflections of mirrors. For hours the king sat lost to the world, shrouded in the dreamy darkness of a grotto, listening to the echoes of a waterfall, surrounded by flowers, trees and shrubs in which a myriad lanterns shone and gaudy parrots swayed on golden perches, while from some hidden source came the sound of music or the bright voice of a court singer, who floated past the entranced king in a gilded skiff over a lake blooming with water-lilies . . .'

Shrubs and flowers sprang up in the audience chambers too, like a thicket guarding an enchanted prince. Visitors were admitted to an empty room, until they discovered to their discomfort that His Majesty was scrutinising them in silence from behind a screen of plants; and at court banquets enormous bouquets of flowers were stationed in front of guests whom the royal host felt obliged to invite but had no desire to see.

By preference he rode out at night, at first to destinations which he reached only in his imagination. Accompanied by a groom, he would climb into the saddle in the evening and continue round and round the riding circuit in the palace grounds until dawn, having completed as many laps as he calculated to be the distance between Munich and Innsbruck or any other town of his fancy.

But more dramatic, often dangerous, were the wild coach dashes at bone-shaking speed from one hunting lodge or castle to another. On summer nights the clatter of his equipage woke the villagers in the Bavarian highlands, in winter the tinkling of sleigh bells and the muffled groan of harness. If they hurried to their windows they might catch a glimpse of outriders with lanterns, footmen with powdered faces, wigs and costumes in the style of Louis Quatorze, behind them a gilt sleigh shaped like a shell in which the monarch sat ensconced – and already the phantom riders had vanished from sight, a will-o'-the-wisp, perhaps only a dream.

The king shrank from his subjects' inquisitive eyes. He had begun to lose his looks. By his late twenties there were unsightly gaps in his front teeth, his handsome face was bloated, he was overweight. Audiences might be cancelled and banquets post-poned, but how should he contrive those visits to the theatre he so loved without being submitted to the public gaze and the rapturous ovations which he found 'more unpleasant than assassinations'?

He instituted royal command performances, for himself alone. In the course of fifteen years over two hundred of these so-called 'separate performances' took place in the Residenz theatre for an audience of one. The auditorium fully lit, the outer vestibule and all the approaching corridors extravagantly ablaze with lights, Ludwig sat alone in the royal box, lorgnon raised to his eye, scrutinising the stage for errors that offended the only standard he thought mattered: perfect historical veracity.

Nearly all the plays he commissioned resurrected the court life of the Bourbon kings Louis Quatorze, Quinze and Seize, his namesakes and his epitomes of absolutist monarchy. What he sought on the stage was not appearance, but reality. And it was in order to give this reality a setting worthy of its protagonists that he set about building a stage of gigantic dimensions – the castles of Linderhof and Herrenchiemsee, his private mausoleums to the memory of the Bourbon kings.

Ludwig began work on Schloß Linderhof at the age of twenty-three, completing it ten years later. It was the first, and the most modest, of the three castles he designed, and it was the only one to be finished during his lifetime. Situated on the Tyrolean border, not far from Oberammergau and Ettal, the country house that went on sprawling until it had eventually become a castle was dubbed by its whimsical architect 'Meicost Ettal', which only the initiated can have recognised as an anagram of 'L'état c'est moi'.

If the architecture and the lavish interior were a celebration of the age of Louis XIV, the eerie cavern known as the Blue Grotto which Ludwig had built in the gardens was pure Wagner: artificial stalactites suspended from the roof, a huge painting of 'Tannhäuser im Venusberg' spanning the background, like a cyclorama, to a waterfall and a lake where the king bathed with swans or drifted dreamily, preferably at night, in a gilded cockle-shell to the accompaniment of delirious ripples of multi-coloured lights. Backstage, a team of sweating labourers stoked the boilers that fired the grotto's central heating, engineers and technicians feverishly grappled with wave-making apparatus or His Majesty's impossible demands for a particular shade of turquoise light.

In 1876 Ludwig travelled by his private train to Bayreuth to attend the inauguration of the Festspielhaus and the first performance of Wagner's tetralogy, the Ring of the Nibelungen. It was his last appearance in public.

He spent the remaining ten years of his life supervising the building of castles in which he would never live for more than a few days or weeks at a stretch. In the middle of the night he sometimes descended on Schloß Linderhof, completed in 1876, simply in order to have a meal before his carriage whisked him away again into the dark.

It became his routine to spend ten days in September every year at his imitation Versailles, the lake island castle of Herrenchiemsee, where he had the two and a half thousand candles lit in the Gallery of Mirrors and stamped up and down, a solitary figure, for hours on end, hurling his legs up and out in that extraordinary affected gait which he believed to have been practised by Louis XIV. Here he dined alone, as in all his castles, at a table which could be lowered into the floor and raised between courses so that His Majesty remained undisturbed by any other human presence. The only dining companions he admitted to his table were ghosts. A place was always laid for two or three invisible guests, eminent representatives of the Versailles court, Madame de Maintenon or the Sun King himself, with whom the Bavarian Louis exchanged toasts and was reported to enjoy animated conversations.

At Neuschwanstein he returned to the Middle Ages. In his imagination it had become a mystical castle, a repository of the Grail, and the interior began to resemble a kind of warehouse of stage sets for Wagnerian opera. Whether in the king's private chambers or the bizarre grotto, the Throne Room or the airy Singers' Hall, built for acoustics that would never be put to the test, here he was surrounded by old friends, Lohengrin and Tristan, Tannhäuser and Parsifal, staring down at him from painted walls.

Ludwig actually inhabited his fantasy castle for no more than about a hundred days. He never held court there or in any of his castles. They were for himself alone. To have taken anyone on a tour of his castles would have been like giving them admittance to his soul.

An increasingly troubled soul, he forbade his servants to look at him. They entered and departed from the royal presence bent at the waist with their eyes on the floor. Those whom he observed snatching an involuntary glimpse of him had to wear a mask as a punishment. A lackey whose stupidity had angered the king carried a seal stamped in wax on his brow as a sign that his brain was likewise sealed. He drank chloral hydrate potions in order to be able to sleep. He began to see and hear things that did not exist.

In the eyes of the country people, the farmers and woodmen in the highland villages who saw much more of the king than did his court or capital, Ludwig could do no wrong. He was at ease with them, talked naturally and took a kindly interest, spontaneously distributed largesse. His popularity was legendary and would always remain so.

But his coffers were now empty. By the summer of 1885 the privy purse groaned under a debt of fifteen million marks. The construction of Neuschwanstein and Herrenchiemsee had to be suspended. The king fretted and fumed. Why this churlish fuss about something as trivial as money? His grandfather had spent as much building his castles, if not more. The thwarting of his still unfinished projects made Ludwig desperate. He ordered emissaries to canvass loans from the shah in Teheran and the sultan in Constantinople, from the kings of the world between Naples and Brazil; he dispatched his servants to Frankfurt to rob Rothschild's bank and planned further bank robberies in Paris and Berlin, but none of these hare-brained schemes were ever put into effect.

A year later his ministers took independent action. Gudden supplied them with an endorsement of the king's commitment on psychiatric grounds, Prince Luitpold was persuaded to step in as regent on behalf of his eccentric nephew, thus providing the necessary political guarantees, and the way was clear for the fateful journey to Neuschwanstein and the final act of Ludwig's life on the shore of Lake Starnberg.

'To drown . . . to sink into unconsciousness . . . the height of pleasure – ' Perhaps the words which this unhappy man wrote to Wagner after a performance of *Tristan* might also serve as his epitaph.

LAMENT FOR THE MAKARIS
In Memory of Richard Burton

R ichard Burton slumped in his chair and surveyed the
wreckage of the dinner table. All of a sudden he seemed
to have become drunk; not by degrees, declining gradually through an evening of Jack Daniels, vodka and tequila, but
precipitately and frighteningly, as if he had fallen over a cliff.

Only two of his guests had stayed the course with him. The
mild-mannered, elderly publicity agent who had flown in from
Los Angeles that afternoon to discuss arrangements for the
forthcoming Academy Awards sat on his left; and on his right,
at the far end of the table, was the young Englishman he had
invited to the family home in Puerto Vallarta in Mexico as private
tutor to the children. The children had slipped away to their
rooms, local guests, rich Americans who wintered in Vallarta,
to their homes. Elizabeth Taylor prowled up and down on the
other side of the room.

'Dunbar!' exclaimed Richard unexpectedly. 'Anybody ever
heard of Dunbar?'

'A late medieval Scottish poet,' responded the tutor, adding
warily, 'but I've never read anything he wrote.'

'Not read Dunbar? Well now, David, I can *recite* him.'

And he could, too. No idle boast. Words that had been
written five hundred years ago surfaced astonishingly through
the drunken torpor of the mind of a Welsh actor sitting on
a balcony overlooking the Pacific, and advanced majestically
down the resonant avenues his voice unfurled in the evening
air. One stanza, a second, a third. The sun seared the horizon

and dipped swiftly into the sea, detonating the sky in a series of gold, pink and vermilion explosions. And after each stanza, the sun down now, the sonorous Latin refrain of Dunbar's poem sounded somehow darker with each repetition.

Timor mortis conturbat me! The fear of death anguishes me! A dozen stanzas, a dozen times the same remorseless, thundering refrain. The voice sank as suddenly and mysteriously as it had arisen, leaving silence and darkness, the memory in eclipse, the light extinguished.

Elizabeth put her hands on her husband's shoulders and said gently, 'I think that's your cue to go to bed.'

Richard got up without a word and allowed himself, stumbling, to be guided up the stairs.

The publicity agent sat motionless in the dark, head in hands, weeping silently. A night breeze crept up off the ocean and ruffled the clusters of shells hanging from the eaves into a sound like the splintering of fine porcelain.

In August 1984 I read a brief notice on the front page of the *Herald Tribune*: Death of Richard Burton, the celebrated actor, in a hospital in Geneva at the age of fifty-nine.

My first reaction on reading the notice of Richard's death was not a feeling but an image: the image of a man reciting Dunbar as he sat on a balcony overlooking the Pacific. For the young tutor from England present on that unforgettable occasion was myself.

Fourteen years ago. Dissolve and flashback. My parents' house in the home counties in England, early in the new year of 1970 . . .

Nevill Coghill, emeritus professor of English literature at Oxford University, and an old friend of the family's, called me up one evening and asked me if I would be interested in a job as private tutor to the children of Richard Burton and Elizabeth Taylor. Yes, I said, I would.

Richard had got to know Nevill at Oxford during the war. It

was Nevill to whom he turned when the education of Elizabeth Taylor's younger son became a pressing concern. He was not satisfied with the education Christopher Wilding was getting in Hawaii, and presented him with an ultimatum: either a boarding school or a private tutor. Christopher opted for the latter. Richard duly wrote to Nevill, asking him to recommend someone.

I accepted the job, not believing it would really happen. I was working as a stage-hand in a Munich theatre at the time. But around the middle of February a voice materialised from the other side of the Atlantic and instructed me to pick up immediately a pre-paid ticket to Los Angeles.

And there, suddenly and wholly improbably, I was, in an enormous suite in the Beverley Hills hotel. The next morning I sat in the Polo Lounge, being briefed by Valerie Douglas, a former secretary of Richard's and now publicity officer at United Artists, on the intricacies of my mission. I watched sleek businessmen confer by telephone over their breakfast. A glass of orange juice cost a dollar. I drank a dollar and was served potted histories of my employers for my breakfast. Phrases like 'at the height of their international love affair' swam nonchalantly in the glittering shoals that issued from Valerie's lips. I must show affection for the dogs, even if I hated dogs. Very important, the dogs. She had brought one along with her, as a sample, from the recent litter of E'en so, Richard's Pekinese bitch with the Shakespearean name. 'Delivered by Caesarean section,' said Valerie. 'A thousand dollars a piece.'

Two days later I slid into the black limousine with the silent chauffeur and tinted glass and was driven to the airport. Rendez-vous with Christopher Wilding and his cousin, Chris Taylor, who had just flown in from Hawaii. The boys were cautious. I was cautious. We would make friends during the flight to Mexico.

A discreet word in my ear as I said goodbye to Valerie Douglas. 'Pick your way carefully, now. You'll find they are a strange bunch down there.'

*

When we stepped out of the air-conditioned plane and into the wall of the humid Mexican night, Swiss-born polyglot Raymond, Elizabeth's personal assistant and Man Friday seven days a week, currently a sort of major domo at Casa Kimberley, was waiting on the tarmac to meet us. The dune buggy took us and our luggage aboard and we rocketed off into the night. It was an exhilarating ride.

On the way to Casa Kimberley I encountered the faces of my employers, a yard high and somewhat hispanicized, on the posters outside the local cinema. They must have been travelling incognito, because they were billed as Antony and Cleopatra.

The car came to a halt at the top of a narrow cobbled street outside a tall, massive-walled house ablaze with lights. We got out. Cayo, the Mexican houseboy, appeared at the door to fetch our luggage.

'Hey, Cayo! Hey, man! Right on!'

The boys frisked and capered, relishing the scent of home.

And then I became aware of something beside all the capering and back-slapping that was going on in the street, above and beyond all that. Twenty feet above, to be precise. I looked up and saw Richard Burton standing in silence, hands in pockets, scrutinising us from the balcony of the house.

Why was there no word of welcome from that impassive figure on the balcony? I felt a sudden chill, our tumbling boisterousness in the street seemed foolish and out of place. By the chemistry of a single glance the scene had been entirely transformed. The brooding figure on the balcony was not Richard Burton, but Heathcliff; I had arrived not at Casa Kimberley but at Wuthering Heights.

At our first meeting he was courteous but reserved, for the most part quite impenetrable. He shook my hand, invited me to call him Richard, at once offered me a drink and escorted me to the bar. I noted a powerful figure, commanding hands, a swollen, pitted face which at some point in his life had assumed a glaze of expressionlessness and slowly petrified into a mask. It betrayed nothing. But of the presence there was not the slightest doubt; a mysterious emanation, which could both draw people and hold them at a distance. I had felt it across twenty feet of darkness. And then there was the voice. I sampled it over the bar. Not just a voice, amplified by pitch and technique, but a marvel of ventriloquism. Even during small talk, with no more space between us than the length of my arm, he sounded like a man addressing me from the bottom of a well. It was always unmistakably Richard's voice which rose up out of that well, but the role in whose service he deployed it was occasionally that of Mark Antony, much more frequently that of Heathcliff, splendid in isolation, not deigning to appear on the set at all.

And what a magnificent set it was, that house overlooking the bay of Puerto Vallarta; a house in two parts, an upper and a lower house, divided by the narrow street. The two houses were connected by a bridge spanning the street. Not any old bridge. It was an exact replica of the Bridge of Sighs in Venice, a sentimental monument to an 'international love affair'.

The lower house, with its bar, sitting room and sun terrace overlooking the swimming pool and a wing for guests, was a later acquisition. When the filming of *The Night of the Iguana* first brought Richard to Puerto Vallarta in the early 1960s there had only been an upper house. Sighs, no doubt, there were already many, but as yet no bridge to give them passage. The lower house was a derelict lot.

In the mornings, when the boys and I were busy in the classroom upstairs, Richard liked to retreat to the lower house to work undisturbed for a couple of hours, accompanied by a portable typewriter. The thoughts that went into this typewriter usually came out of it in the form of tightly crumpled balls of paper. Once, indiscreetly, I smoothed out a piece of this mental litter and discovered with a shock that it was blank.

At noon the typewriter accompanied Richard back across the Bridge of Sighs into the main room of the upper house. There it sat on a stool in front of a chair, paperless and silent. But apparently Richard liked to have it around him. It went wherever he did, jealously guarded by his Pekinese bitch, E'en so. Among all his wealth, his yachts, houses, cars and wardrobes of clothes, it was probably one of the few objects for which he felt any enduring affection.

The main room of the upper house was the centre piece of the Casa Kimberley set. Here the family ate, drank, relaxed, entertained, traded the talk of the day, recited Shakespeare or declaimed Dunbar. A profusion of broad-leaved plants, an almost sensuous vegetation whose green set off the brilliant colours of a prodigal scattering of silk cushions, a balcony always open to light and air and a superb view of the mountains soaring up out of the ocean, gave a sense of space and brightness that never failed to fill my heart with exuberance.

A couple of steps led up from the main room to an open courtyard that swallowed the sun. It was flanked on one side by Raymond's suite, on the other by the rooms occupied by myself and the boys. However extravagant they might appear in public, my employers gave evidence in their private lives of tastes that were discreet to the point of understatement.

Leading off the main room was another flight of stairs, which I ascended only once during the three months I stayed in the house. The stairs led up to Richard's and Elizabeth's room.

It was a small, modest room, the only one that was air-conditioned, but otherwise little different from any of the other rooms. It gave out on to a tiny terrace, where the master and mistress of Casa Kimberley could sunbathe undisturbed and explore, at last, having climbed so many, many stairs, such shreds of intimacy as were left them after the mauling of a cruelly inquisitive world.

I found a certain symbolism in the geography of that house. Richard Burton inhabited the room at the top. It was a pinnacle. And it was recognised as a pinnacle, at least in part, some would say very large part, on account of the woman who shared it with him.

On 27 February 1970, a few days after my arrival, Elizabeth celebrated her thirty-eighth birthday. Her husband was forty-four. Both man and wife were in their prime. At the point when I came briefly into their lives they had been married for six years, having first met on the set of *Cleopatra* in 1961. The marriage was to last for ten years. After the divorce in 1974 they remarried within a year – a last flicker of the Burton-Taylor fire before it finally went out.

At thirty-eight Elizabeth could perhaps no longer contest the claim to be the most beautiful woman in the world as effortlessly as she had once done, but a quarter of a century after she had ridden to international stardom in a film called *National Velvet* she was still sensational to look at.

She was a mature beauty, and that is not a disparaging euphemism. I admired her grace, her flair, the violet coloured eyes in her dark complexion, her sensual femininity. There was something gypsy-like about her. The personality was attractive – forthcoming, frank, and completely natural. In a woman as celebrated for her beauty as she was it surprised me to find almost no evidence of vanity. She would change her outfit several times a day; she liked to present her attractions. But that was not vanity. She simply enjoyed it. It was fun.

For her birthday I gave her some hand-beaten brass earrings which I bought for a few dollars from a local craftsman. She was genuinely delighted and put them on at once. The hands she raised to attach them to her ears were studded with gems worth hundreds of thousands of dollars. I was aware of the absurdity of the contrast, but I don't think she gave it a second thought.

She wore her fame lightly, like a second skin. She never gave me the impression of having to live up to something, as I felt in Richard's case.

Elizabeth's fame was one of the things Richard had to live up to. He did so by giving her presents, which acquired their own notoriety. The Burton-Taylor diamonds made headlines, and I know that one diamond was the subject of a bet – Richard gave it to Elizabeth after losing a point against her during a game of table tennis. The world's most precious lady deserved the most precious stones. In Richard's eyes, the eyes of a boy of humble Welsh origins, those diamonds reflected something more: that he was a partner worthy of Elizabeth Taylor.

As in many marriages, the love had been grafted to a family affair, to a common interest in their children. Richard cared for the children Elizabeth had brought into the marriage as if they had been his own. He was very much a family man. He spoke often and affectionately of Kate, his daughter by his first wife.

Elizabeth's oldest child, Michael Wilding, was away in India at the time, but all the other children came to stay with their parents in Casa Kimberley. Christopher Wilding and his cousin remained there for as long as Richard and Elizabeth were in Mexico. Liza Todd, Elizabeth's third child, came over from school in Europe during the Easter holidays. So did the fourth child, the Burtons' adopted daughter, Maria.

The bond the diamonds symbolised in public relied in private on the love they shared for this daughter. With the help of the skills of an Oxford surgeon the child who had been physically handicapped since infancy had grown into a sturdy, attractive little girl. Perhaps Richard and Elizabeth no longer had very much to say to each other as man and wife, but what they had lost as lovers was compensated for by what they had gained as parents.

Because of her own playful nature it was Elizabeth who became the children's obvious companion during the holidays. It was she who romped with them in the pool, arranged for the deep freeze to be stocked with hamburgers and handed out photograph negatives through which they could view an eclipse of the sun. Her vitality, her immediacy, inspired the children with a sense of fun. Richard did not have that immediacy; he had staying power. His qualities emerged over distance and time. Thus it was Richard who wrote the letters to the boys after they had left Mexico, Elizabeth who added the postcripts.

I liked all the children. They were completely unspoilt. I got to know the two Christophers best. In his character the nephew was more like Elizabeth than the son: impulsive, outgoing, his temperament as suntanned as his skin. His talk was all of coral, surf and lagoons. He reminded me of a splendid, untamed animal.

Christopher Wilding was a more withdrawn, pensive boy. Even his paler skin seemed to have retreated from direct contact with the sun. Perhaps he had already undergone enough exposure in his life.

The children supplied the lynch-pin of Richard's and Elizabeth's marriage. In that respect it was a conventional marriage. It was not hard to predict that when the children left home the marriage would break up. In that respect their marriage was also nothing unusual. They were, after all, only human.

Not long after Elizabeth's birthday a fishing expedition was arranged for all the family, the first of only five or six occasions during my three-month stay when Richard and Elizabeth ventured out of the house at all.

As he walked down the wharf to the moorings of the hired motor boat Richard turned to me and asked 'What's the Spanish for "Is this boat for us?"'

Richard advanced down the gangplank and delivered his line with a conquistador's flourish. The Mexican crew bowed in mute amazement.

As if that boat could have been for anyone other than us. An entire village had laid down tools to watch the royal progress of the party, laden with the equipage of hampers, hat boxes, crates of liquor and sun lotion which were indispensable whenever the Burton-Taylor circus travelled.

On the way out from Vallarta we cruised along the shore of the peninsula where *The Night of the Iguana* had been filmed. The original set, a village specially built for the film, still appeared to be intact, although it had remained uninhabited since.

Richard perked up when he saw the village and related a few anecdotes. This led on to a discussion of fame. Didn't he, I asked tentatively, find that constant exposure to the public eye was rather a two-edged honour?

'Well,' he replied, 'I recently discovered what it's like *not* to be the object of public attention. On location in eastern Europe I found myself having to wait in a queue – something I've not done for as long as I can remember. People didn't recognise me. They hadn't seen my films.'

'Wasn't that rather nice for a change, not being recognised as a celebrity?'

'No. I hated it.'

At dinner that evening Richard got very drunk. Talking of Wales, and perhaps with more respect for Dylan Thomas in his head than respect for agricultural fact, he tossed out the phrase 'fecund fields'.

Elizabeth gave a snort. 'Fecund! Ha!'

Richard turned to me and said coldly 'Elizabeth has a very limited vocabulary, David. That's one of the differences between us. I have an immense vocabulary.'

Elizabeth still wouldn't let go. 'Fecund, for Christ's sake!'

She stalked out of the room. Alone at the table, Richard and I indulged in a little patter on the subject of literature. It wasn't hard to guess that Dylan Thomas was one of Richard's heroes. In Los Angeles I had picked up a slim volume that Richard had published; a story about a Christmas in Wales, I seem to remember. It was not untalented, but it was pastiche, written on Richard's portable typewriter, with Dylan Thomas guiding his fingers to the keys.

I told Richard frankly my opinion of his book.

'Oh, but that's dreadful, David. You shouldn't have bothered to read it.'

And he steered the conversation back to poetry and another of his anecdotes about Dylan. I thought Dylan was splendid, I said, but I had more respect for T S Eliot.

'Eliot? I once met him at a party. Dylan was there too. Eliot said nothing. Dylan upstaged him all the time. There was no way he could compete with Dylan in the same room.'

Richard used the word 'upstaging' on another occasion, some months later, after he had been to see Richardson and Gielgud in David Storey's play *Home*.

'It was marvellous,' he said affectionately, 'to watch those two old codgers upstaging one another.' That was his only comment on the play.

Upstaging was a key word in Richard Burton's immense vocabulary. A powerful man and a powerful actor, he had always been good at it himself. Critics had noted this aspect of his talent, not with approval, in the early 1950s. It had been known to jeopardise a production.

And up there, in the room at the top, on that pinnacle of success, it was the same issue that teased his marriage. All efforts to upstage Elizabeth Taylor were doomed to failure. Richard might send out as many invitations as he liked with Mr & Mrs Richard Burton printed at the head of the card, but it was Mr & Mrs Taylor whom the majority of the guests wanted to come and see.

It was no coincidence that all the house guests came from Britain. David Frost, in transit with a dizzy blonde, Brook Williams (Emlyn's son) and his wife Liz, Norma Heyman and the children's tutor – the sun terraces of Casa Kimberley were packed with national allies.

Elizabeth's views on formal education were vague. It was Richard who took the matter in hand. The tutor had to be someone from Oxford. Nobody else would do. Howard Taylor,

Elizabeth's brother, shared his sister's casualness. He wired an inquiry about the tutor's surfing qualifications. Reply negative. Well, never mind. He agreed to let his son accompany Christopher Wilding to Mexico to share the ordeal of an English tutorship.

But beyond the classroom and the sun terraces, where the little principality of Casa Kimberley was assured a sort of diplomatic immunity, lay the American continent. Camera teams were flown in to Vallarta from Los Angeles for an interview, overlooking in their excitement the formality of applying for a working visa, and had to fly home again with empty reels. And when an emissary arrived with an invitation from a minister in the Mexican government, which he presented with florid Latin courtesy, there can have been no doubt as to whom the caballero particularly had in mind. A Mexican airforce plane, suitably camouflaged for such a delicate mission, was already waiting on the tarmac of Vallarta airport to conduct the distinguished guests, whenever, at their gracious convenience . . .

The plane waited for a week.

I asked Richard's secretary, canny Jim Benton, what it was all about.

'Oh, there's a development project in hand,' he said vaguely.

'Development project?'

'Just an excuse. They're star struck, that's all.'

A week later a tired-looking pilot brought a hot plane down on to a sandy airstrip in the jungle. The minister who had issued the original invitation was mysteriously indisposed, but his son Carlos, a massive young man with a hook nose, was waiting to greet the guests on his father's behalf. He didn't get much beyond his father's name, either, because Carlos spoke not a word of English.

The party was paddled across a lagoon in a convoy of six canoes.

'Would you like to have this lagoon?' inquired Carlos through an interpreter.

'How sweet of you,' said Elizabeth.

On the far side of the lagoon we climbed a knoll overlooking the beach and the thunderous surf.

'I thought you might like to build a house here,' said Carlos. 'The land will be a gift, of course. Really, as much as you like . . .' He gestured vaguely towards the horizon.

At the bottom of the knoll a truck was waiting beside a posse of horses. We were given a choice of motorised or four-legged transport on the final stage of the journey to the ranch where Carlos had invited us to lunch.

National Velvet. Carlos had done his homework. Before getting up into the saddle Elizabeth plucked the rings from her fingers and placed her portable Fort Knox nonchalantly in the palm of my hand.

'Just hold on to these for me, will you David?'

I reeled.

'I wouldn't mind a ride either,' said Richard, a shade testily. He was being upstaged.

Meanwhile I was exploring the pockets of my jeans to find out if they had a hole. No. I climbed gingerly into the back of the truck. The Mexicans grinned.

And off we went. The road led through an endless plantation. I asked the interpreter, who was standing beside me in the flatbed, how much land belonged to the estate.

'Ten thousand hectares.'

I knew almost nothing about Mexican politics, but I did happen to know that the middle letter of the initials PRI, the name of the party in power at the time, stood for Revolutionary. I wondered for whose benefit that revolution was being fought. Carlos, for one. That was clear.

But not the Burtons. To their credit they were not going to let themselves be dangled as bait for the fat cats Carlos was hoping would invest in his scheme for a millionaires' paradise along his private stretch of coast. The Burtons didn't say so in as many words, but sorry, Carlos, that was the message.

Carlos, not by nature a very forthcoming man, now disappeared altogether behind a mask of silence, increasing his already marked resemblance to a stone effigy.

Over the marinated fish hors d'oeuvre Elizabeth burbled on enthusiastically about a fantastic white horse she had spotted from the air. The interpreter burbled in hot pursuit. Carlos laid down his fork and issued a terse instruction to the henchman standing beside his chair. He did not eat much. His eyes, and apparently his appetite, were entirely at the disposal of his charming guests.

They had now emerged, scathed, from a labyrinth of broiled fish and roast meats, and were staggering towards the exit of their lunch when the henchman sidled back into the room and sought the favour of his master's ear. This time Carlos did not lay down his fork. He picked it up, and jabbing it in the direction of the henchman's face pronounced sotto voce a verdict that must have been close to a sentence of death, for I have never seen the colour drain from someone's face so fast. Richard must have thought the same thing too. He caught my eyes across the table and raised an eyebrow inquiringly. But Carlos reassured us with an expansive smile. A mere trifle. Would we care for coffee, brandy and cigars?

When the company rose from the table at the end of lunch the white horse admired by Elizabeth at the beginning had been identified by an air patrol sent out on Carlos' orders, separated from the herd by cowboys informed by radio of its whereabouts, lassooed and ridden back to the ranch, where it could now be viewed grazing in a paddock behind the house.

There was only one problem. The animal might look fine from the air, but on closer inspection it turned out that its ribs were showing through its mangy flanks. Carlos could not present so noble a horsewoman with so wretched a mount. He would feel highly honoured if she would accept his own white stallion instead.

Elizabeth accepted. She would have been foolish not to. The

hospitality of Carlos was not extended as an invitation, but as a command. We were all terrified of him.

So no objections were raised when Carlos suggested we fly on to his 'apartment' in Guadalajara, and we were not a bit surprised when the apartment revealed itself to be a palace set in spacious grounds. It became difficult to express recognition of our host's fabulous generosity when a careless word of praise for anything we saw meant to be encumbered with it instantly as an incontestable gift. Elizabeth acquired a second horse, with a magnificent silver-inlaid saddle for the first, and Richard only narrowly averted a peacock.

Ten silent admirers of Mr & Mrs Burton, all of them male, attended a sepulchral palace feast and sat waiting for the oracles to speak. But Elizabeth was not playing. She had had quite enough for one day. Whether it was the atmosphere in that mausoleum of a dining-room, or a vein of tedium vitae that nourished Richard's memory with so many funereal quotations, or merely a mischievous impulse, whatever – he suddenly launched off on the subject of poet laureates.

It was not the most obvious conversational gambit. Ten Mexican grandees, all of them with glowing eyes, none of them with the benefit of English, cannot have been much enlightened.

'Poor fellows, the rubbish they've been forced to write. Royal hacks, maybe, but still hacks. A specimen of which I'm particularly fond is the couplet on the approaching death of George the Fifth, or was it the Sixth?

> 'Along the electric wires the message came:
> The king's condition is still the same.'

We both cracked up, exploding the dreadful solemnity of that room, and in that moment we became allies.

It was only by a hair's breadth that our allegiance survived the day. Richard strolled out through Guadalajara after dinner, escorted by tough-looking caballeros toting machine guns.

Returning in the small hours after a raucous night on the town, I benefited from the same watchfulness, but unfortunately at the wrong end of the barrel.

Failing to get any response by ringing the palace bell, I shinned up its superable walls instead. Perhaps a bit risky, I reflected too late, just as I heard the sound of a rifle being cocked. I looked down to see a soldier who had detached himself from the shadow of a tree and was now taking aim at me in the moonlight. Only the presence of mind of the minister's chauffeur, waiting at the kerb to see me safely in, spared Carlos the embarrassment of one of his guests being shot by one of his palace guards.

However grotesque the Carlos episode might appear to me, it was probably nothing out of the ordinary for my employers. In her heyday it could be said of Elizabeth Taylor, as it was once allegedly said of Napoleon, that she extended the boundaries of fame. It was a hard act to follow, and nobody can have been more aware of that than Richard Burton.

Throughout March the heavy drinking continued. While the sun shone brilliantly outside, monsoon weather in Casa Kimberley. On one evening Richard was in such a bad state that Elizabeth asked me to keep the boys occupied outside the house for a couple of hours.

She began to take me into her confidence. There were few places in that airy, open house where confidences could be exchanged, and thus it came about that she and I were sometimes closeted in the cloakroom of the lower house. We were once discovered there by Richard, who had come down to fetch his beloved typewriter and overheard our voices.

'Who's that in there?' he boomed, Hamlet this time, challenging his father's ghost.

'It's me,' replied the tutor's ghost. 'I'm in here with Elizabeth.'

'Elizabeth? What? *My* Elizabeth?'

He never brought the subject up afterwards.

Farce threatened to curdle tragedy. Any further conversations on the premises became impossible. Elizabeth suggested an outing to her private beach instead, with her son Christopher making up a threesome, to prevent unnecessary gossip. Transport to the beach posed the main problem. The white dune buggy had itself become a celebrity along the entire coast. An alternative was parked under the Bridge of Sighs – Raymond's Volkswagen, but this was an almost sacred vehicle.

'He's so fussy about that car. D'you think we can ask him to lend it to us?'

Raymond gave Elizabeth his permission.

While Christopher wandered along the beach in search of shells, his mother talked about her marriage. She loved her husband. But did he love her? She worried that she was losing him. She had doubts about herself. When she called herself 'an old bag' she was not fishing for compliments. I was quite convinced of her sincerity.

'The trouble is,' she said sadly, 'I think I just bore him.'

I would have put the problem differently. The trouble was that Richard bored himself.

Richard did not disclose his feelings in the way that Elizabeth did. He was not a disclosing kind of man. Instead he sent out signals, a code which I had to learn to read. Since the outing to Guadalajara I felt that he had now become accustomed to my presence around the house, and in fact wanted my companionship.

Playing pool was one form of companionship. Richard played a good game of pool, perhaps very good, when one considers he often played it drunk, was frequently interrupted by tourists whose hands he reeled downstairs to shake through the bars of the house gate, and still beat me easily.

Scrabble was another. Scrabble had to be played sober, because here I offered more serious opposition. We both liked to play strictly by the rules. That was another point in common. Whatever wasn't in the Oxford English Dictionary - and there it stood, of course, all twelve volumes of it - wasn't allowed.

Richard beat me at Scrabble, too, which I minded more than losing at pool.

Scrabble symbolised the code; the knowledge of words and the appreciation of literature. Richard did not tell people he was in distress. He got drunk and recited Dunbar instead. His idea of fun was not to put plastic frogs inside my swimming trunks, as Elizabeth was quite likely to do, but to discuss with me the possibility of translating together Sartre's play *Le Diable et le bon Dieu*, The Devil and the good Lord. Richard wanted to play the devil.

He had an immoderate respect for academic learning. It was characteristic that the only anecdote - and he was a man of very many anecdotes - which Richard told me about Marlon Brando was that he had taught himself Greek.

My first impression of Richard was that he was an intellectual snob, arrogant, bombastic, given to pedantry. But he was not a snob or a pedant. He posed as one. He put intellectual snobbery up in front of himself as a screen, proving to himself and the world that he still had serious standards and ambitions, which in private he feared he was losing or had already lost altogether.

Intellectualism disguised nostalgia. He was a Welshman right down to the bottom of that extraordinary well of a voice, but he was not merely a Welshman and the Welsh influence, assiduously cultivated, was not of course the only one. Oxford was not in Wales, nor was Stratford or the Old Vic; his epitomes of academic and theatrical excellence. These places were his intellectual homes. Richard had wanted to return to Oxford after the war, but, as he said, 'instead I became what, for want of a better word, is known as a star.'

Having embarked on his career as a star, for want of a better life, Richard reorientated his ambition according to the standards by which movie stars are judged. He must acquire not only the attributes of stardom, the wealth and the notoriety. He must also be crowned with the laurel of Hollywood's formal acclaim. He must win an Oscar.

So far the Oscar had eluded his grasp. He had been nominated several times, without success.

The savage bout of drinking throughout that March culminated in his recital of Dunbar's refrain: the fear of death anguishes me! The next morning he went on the wagon, and a week later, still aboard, he was rolling north to Los Angeles for the presentation of the Academy Awards.

He had been nominated for his performance in *Anne of the Thousand Days*. Among the other contestants in 1970 were Jon Voigt, Dustin Hoffman, Peter O'Toole and John Wayne. Richard was relieved of the burden of at least one extra piece of luggage on the journey to LA. His wife had not been nominated that year. No potential rivalry there.

John Wayne won, but Richard didn't lose. He did not regard it as a defeat, as he might have done in the case of Dustin Hoffman, certainly if he had gone down to O'Toole. Good old John Wayne, ten foot tall, great Hollywood character, loyal servant of the film industry, receives his just reward. Richard accepted the decision with good grace. His condescending interpretation of the criteria for the Academy's decision allowed his self-esteem to slip past unbruised. And besides, he had accomplished something more important than the Oscar. He was still on the wagon.

I am glad, before our ways parted, to have seen what Richard could be like when he was off the booze. He was a transformed man. Perhaps it was the best transformation of his career. The ease and naturalness with which he played a sober part convinced me of Richard's qualities as a man. The moody Heathcliff, the swaggering Antony, were troubled phantoms, released from the bottle like evil djinn. His face cleared, his eyes brightened, he talked better, began to take more interest in things. And for the first time I saw that he was indeed, underneath the mask of booze, still a very fine-looking man.

The code language continued, but the signals were more encouraging now. Two large volumes, not on the tutor's list of books Jim Benton had flown in from America, were presented to me after a marathon Scrabble session in which I had beaten Richard by a couple of points: the compact edition of the OED. Richard's generosity was always discreet, the result of careful appraisal of the recipient's needs.

How else could it have occurred to him to give me the Senior Sportsman slingshot? He must have remembered me admiring it in the hands of someone demonstrating it on the beach. As he handed me the dictionary and the slingshot Richard commented that both, in their different ways, would prove better aids to accuracy.

Without fuss he took in his stride a number of inconveniences I caused. When I lost my key in a Vallarta night club – a master key that would open all of Casa Kimberley's very private doors – he footed the bill to have the locks changed throughout the house, without a murmur. And when I snapped off the dune buggy's perforated gear shift while attempting a racing change on a sharp corner he only remarked how shoddy so much workmanship had become these days. He paid for the damage I'd done. More importantly, he put me at my ease.

We all went out dancing – Richard, Elizabeth, the whole family. A month before it would have been inconceivable. I don't think the two of them had been out dancing in years, for their own benefit rather than for the onlookers. Dancing days, happy days, practical jokes and pranks in the main room of the upper house. Although still abstinent himself, Richard used to mix me devastating martinis, which was rather like a pyromaniac constructing fire bombs for someone else to throw.

They were quite something, those martinis. On one occasion they transformed me into a matador and Elizabeth into a bull. She was a very fiery bull, and a courageous one, too, for I was equipped with real banderillas, souvenirs of a corrida we had just seen in Guadalajara. Richard played the arena and ten thousand spectators, without exaggeration a monumental part.

A final cameo from a strange, eventful history that already

seemed unreal. Cameras off. The tigerish month of May, the season of fierce heat, had arrived in Mexico, bringing silence to Casa Kimberley. The two Christophers and I left for Europe, where my year as their tutor would be completed. Richard and Elizabeth for other locations, other films, in which I would no longer play a part.

Ours wasn't finished yet, however. I had seen the rushes of Richard Burton on the Casa Kimberley set. They were fine as far as they went, but there was still some editing to do.

The Dunbar verses Richard Burton so memorably recited came from a poem called 'Lament for the Makaris'– an obsolete word meaning 'makers', in this case poets. It is an elegy, mourning the transitoriness of the world, the ephemerality of life in general and the poets who were Dunbar's predecessors in particular, one of whom was Chaucer.

I don't know where Richard first became acquainted with this poem, but a fair guess would be Oxford. In that case there can be little doubt as to who it was that brought the poem to his attention: Nevill Coghill. Coghill was an authority on medieval literature, notably on Chaucer. It was Coghill who published a modern English version of Chaucer and made *The Canterbury Tales* a box-office success on the London stage.

If one traces the associations back in this way I think it becomes possible to explain why this 'Lament for the Makaris' should have remained so obstinately in the forty-four-year-old Richard Burton's memory. I think he was reciting his own lament, not for the things that had departed from his world (for they were still there), but for the things on which, in retrospect mistakenly, he had himself turned his back.

It was not the fear of death, which anguished Richard Burton. It was the fear that he had betrayed his own talent. Or had it betrayed him?

At quite a late stage in his relatively short life, in reply to a question about why his theatre appearances had become so rare, he said, 'I think I'm afraid.'

One recalls the glowing testimonials of his early career. 'This boy of genius,' noted Nevill Coghill in 1944. After his Stratford season in 1951 Richard Burton was proclaimed to be 'the *one*, he was the crown prince, he was the actor who would take the mantle of both Gielgud and Olivier.'

Three years later his performance as Coriolanus at the Old Vic was judged to have taken him 'a sturdy stride nearer the greatness that so surely lies ahead of him'. Philip Burton, the drama teacher who had given his protégé Richard Jenkins the name under which he became famous, also saw that performance. 'He was the definitive Coriolanus, and Olivier agreed with me.'

Laurence Olivier was the standard by which critics had once measured the young Richard Burton. Richard also saw himself as taking the Greatest Actor's mantle, but with a self-knowledge that was denied his admirers he described his fitness to be Olivier's successor in very much more modest terms. 'I'm really the poor man's Olivier.'

Olivier, Olivier. The name became a burden and an obsession. 'If you're going to make rubbish, be the best rubbish in it. That's what I keep telling Larry Olivier.'

Which Olivier was he telling? Larry? Or the poor man's Olivier?

The poor man's Olivier was offered and accepted the part of Antony in *Cleopatra*. Larry Olivier was offered the part of Caesar, and declined.

Larry Olivier did not take his poor relation's advice. He is alleged to have offered him his own instead. 'You've got to choose whether you want to be an actor or a household name.'

Richard was himself well aware of the choice.

'Everybody's offered a choice: one easy, one difficult. Most men, regardless of their craft, profession or background, are faced at one time or another with an obvious, easy one and a difficult, more rewarding one.'

Richard made his choice. There was not much Olivier left in the poor man's Olivier at the end.

Richard Burton was well established on his way to stardom before I was born. I saw him perform on the stage only once. Nevill Coghill coaxed him back to the Oxford Playhouse for what by 1966 had become a very rare theatre appearance. He agreed to play the title part in Marlowe's play *The Tragical History of Dr Faustus*.

Marlowe's *Faustus* (as Goethe's later *Faust*) is based on a medieval legend about a man who sells his soul to the devil in exchange for universal knowledge, worldly riches and power. The devil gratifies all his desires, and at Faustus' bidding even summons up the apparition of Helen of Troy. Satiated by all these marvels, but still strangely unsatisfied, Faustus faces the hour when the devil will fetch him to damnation. He repents, but his repentance comes too late.

Richard Burton offered journalists his comments on the role: 'I've been wanting to play Faustus for more than twenty years. I know the part, but not as well as I thought. A lot of Marlowe's lines started coming out as Burton's lines.'

Dr Faustus was renowned for his learning in the art of black magic; an ambiguous gift, for it was the art of black magic that gave him access to the devil. Richard Burton practised his own kind of magic with a naturally compelling presence, a naturally marvellous voice. But was this magic a reliable substitute for the solid foundation of technique?

As early as 1948 the distinguished critic C A Lejeune, Ken Tynan's predecessor in the theatre column of the *Observer*, remarked how the young Richard Burton had 'a trick of getting the maximum effect with the minimum of fuss'.

And Burton himself was once quoted as saying, 'I could go to Scunthorpe to act in repertory for nothing; admirable, maybe, but an exercise.'

Exercise? He disparaged it.

In 1981 I worked on a studio recording with Anthony Quayle in London. Quayle knew Richard intimately from their years together in Stratford during the early 1950s. He told me how he had once invited Richard to join him for a repertory season; the experience, he suggested, would help to improve his technique.

Richard declined the invitation. 'I'm afraid,' he explained to Quayle, 'that technique would interfere with what is my real asset – a knack. I just have a knack, you see.'

He did indeed. He had the knack of the devil.

Richard played on two tables and lost on both: no Oscar for the obvious, easy choice and no knighthood for the difficult, more rewarding one.

Gradually we lost touch. There was a brief meeting at the Dorchester, followed by a visit to watch him on location when he was filming *Villain* in London. A year later a lunch together at a studio in Munich. He wrote a few letters. He was a very loyal friend. I gave up my theatre ambitions and went to Japan, in search of another enigma. It was not time or distance that separated us. We were separated by his fame. He again became someone whom I heard of only in newspaper headlines.

The *Herald Tribune*. Death of Richard Burton, actor, aged fifty-nine.

The private film which we had made together in Mexico could now be given a title: *The Tragical History of Richard Burton*.